AMERICA'S BEST TAX STRATEGIES

AMERICA'S BEST TAX STRATEGIES

Legitimate Ways To Save Income Taxes Now

Stephen D. Kirkland, CPA

To order additional copies of this book, contact:
Xlibris Corporation
1-888-795-4274
www.Xlibris.com
Orders@Xlibris.com
26899

CONTENTS

Acknowledgements 9
Forward 11
Important Note 13
The Power of Tax-Free Compounding 15
The Strategies 17
    Bonds 17
    Tax Deferred Annuities 20
    The Roth IRA 25
    Investing for Education 28
    412(i) Plans 31
    Owners Only 401(k) 33
    Private Pensions 37
    Selling Assets Through A VUL 41
    Life Insurance Trusts 44
    Donating an Appreciated Asset 46
    Charitable Remainder Trusts 48
    Homeownership 52
    Business Use of the Home 56
    Vacation Homes 60
    Rental Real Estate 63
    Segregating Costs 70
    The Family Farm 72
    Conservation Easements 77
    Like-Kind Exchanges of Real Estate 79
    Housing Credits 88
    Private Annuities 91
    Captive Insurance Companies 96
    The U.S. Virgin Islands
        Economic Development 102

Long-Term Care Coverage 106
Frequent Flyer Miles 109
Business Autos 111
Employing Family 116
Leveraging Equity.. 117
Benefiting From State Apportionment 121

Terminology and Concepts...................................... 125
The Double Taxation Dilemma 127
Planning for Capital Gains 133
Important Words of Caution 136
Should We Have a Flat Tax? 139
Would a National Sales Tax be a Better Tax? 143
Asset Protection 148
Updates.. 152
Some Final Thoughts 153
About Moore Kirkland & Beauston L.L.P. 154
Index 155

Dedication

This book is gratefully dedicated to America's veterans, whose sacrifices have defended human rights around the globe and made it possible for Americans to live freely in the greatest country in the world.

Acknowledgements

Preparation of this book was indeed a team effort. Many members of Moore Kirkland & Beauston L.L.P. diligently assisted with the research, drafting and editing.

The insight and research of a few people must be acknowledged because they contributed so greatly to the timely completion of this work: Frank D. Thomas, CPA, CVA; Starlene W. Watson, CPA, CSEP; Darin J. Aldinger, CPA; Mark J. Swanson, CPA, CVA and James Kelley.

We also appreciate the support of family, clients and friends.

Forward

Why does America have tax strategies? The reason is quite simple. Congress has always liked using the Internal Revenue Code to encourage (or discourage) desired behavior. This is sometimes referred to as "social engineering." Our Congress also uses incentives in the tax laws to steer the economy, encourage conservation, and to achieve other objectives.

For example, Congress wanted landowners to plant seedlings, so they created the reforestation credit. They needed employers to provide group health insurance to their employees, so they created tax breaks for those who do. To encourage support of public charities, Congress created many significant tax benefits for those who donate. The list goes on. And that is one reason why the Internal Revenue Code (IRC) and Regulations are now more than seven million words long.

From the taxpayers' standpoint, these incentives are tax strategies. Taking advantage of them is simply fulfilling the desires of Congress.

But who would be interested in using tax strategies? According to the Congressional Joint Economic Committee, the federal income tax burden is borne by a relatively small group of Americans. In fact, they say that one percent of the American population pays 34 percent of the personal income taxes collected by the IRS.

Five percent of our population pays 53 percent of the

federal income taxes. And ten percent pays 65 percent of the taxes.

Fifty percent of our population pays 96 percent of the taxes. Anyone in that fifty percent has plenty of reason to consider every legitimate tax strategy.

This book describes some of the incentives, or tax strategies, that could defer or eliminate a portion of your tax burden. So, take advantage of those that are available, but remember that there are *always* limits to any tax benefit. Ask plenty of questions before you dive into any investment or tax strategy. Consult with your tax advisor to be sure you understand how it all applies to your particular situation.

Also, remember that timing and documentation are always important considerations in tax planning. As one nutty professor used to say, 50% of tax planning is timing and the other 90% is documentation.

Important Note

This book is designed to provide helpful information to be used in legitimate tax planning. This information should be used in conjunction with, and not as a substitute for, professional advice. Each taxpayer has a unique set of facts. Every tax rule has exceptions. The laws (and interpretation of laws) may change at any time.

Due to the complexity of the tax laws, it is not wise to self-diagnose or to self-medicate. Instead, develop a close working relationship with a reputable tax advisor. Be sure he or she is willing to invest the substantial amount of time required throughout the year to keep current with the rapidly-changing federal and state tax laws.

Check with your tax advisor *before* each transaction. Seek a second opinion if you are uncomfortable, and ask for advice on significant issues to be provided to you in writing.

Choose the members of your financial team wisely, and don't be afraid to pay for good advice. It will save you money in the long run. Introduce your CPA to your attorney, financial planner, investment advisor, insurance agent and banker. Give them permission to discuss your confidential matters with each other. And encourage them to work together, since a team can accomplish much more than individuals.

Focus on the three key factors that must be addressed to complete any tax strategy: the timing of the transactions, keeping adequate documentation, and proper reporting. Don't focus entirely on the federal tax and forget to consider the state tax impact. And be wary of the traps that catch so many people, such as the passive loss rules, basis limitations, and the #&%$@* alternative minimum tax!

Also, please remember that tax planning is an ongoing process, not an annual event. As with other areas of financial planning, a strategy that suits you well now may not meet your needs in a few months.

Although not every strategy discussed in this book will fit your situation, at least six or seven of them will. Discuss them with your financial advisors soon. The sooner you get started, the sooner you'll be back on the golf course where you belong.

The Power of
Tax-Free Compounding

What's the difference between $107 million and $279,000? Would you believe the difference is taxes?

Take a good look at the following chart. You will see two columns of compounding numbers. In each column, a dime is invested on the first day of a month. The investment is doubled every day during that month.

The only difference between the two columns is that daily gains in the first column are not taxed, but each daily gain in the second column is taxed at the rate of 36%.

Of course, the idea that you can double your investment every day for a month is a little far fetched, unless you know something the rest of us don't know. But this chart illustrates the power of compounding, and the dramatic effect taxes have on your investment returns. That's why tax planners recommend you put as much as possible into tax free, or tax deferred, vehicles such as annuities and IRAs. The impact of taxes may be just as important to your investments as liquidity and rate of return.

The Power of Tax-Free Compounding

A Dime Doubled Every Day For a Full Month

Days	Tax Free	36% Tax
1	$ 0.10	$ 0.10
2	0.20	0.16
3	0.40	0.27
4	0.80	0.44
5	1.60	0.72
6	3.20	1.19
7	6.40	1.95
8	12.80	3.19
9	25.60	5.23
10	51.20	8.58
11	102.40	14.07
12	204.80	23.08
13	409.60	37.86
14	819.20	62.08
15	1,638.40	101.82
16	3,276.80	166.98
17	6,553.60	273.84
18	13,107.20	449.10
19	26,214.40	736.53
20	52,428.80	1,207.91
21	104,857.60	1,980.97
22	209,715.20	3,248.78
23	419,430.40	5,328.01
24	838,860.80	8,737.93
25	1,677,721.60	14,330.20
26	3,355,443.20	23,501.53
27	6,710,886.40	38,542.51
28	13,421,772.80	63,209.72
29	26,843,545.60	103,663.95
30	53,687,091.20	170,008.87
31	$ 107,374,182.40	$ 278,814.55

The Strategies

Bonds

Municipal bonds and U.S. Savings bonds are one of the safest tax-advantaged investments.

Municipal bonds are readily available and can earn interest that is exempt from both federal and state income taxes. (You have to love that tax-free income!)

A municipal bond will pay interest at a set rate on a regular schedule. The interest is exempt from federal income tax, although interest from certain bonds may be subject to the alternative minimum tax. The interest could be exempt from state income tax as well, if your bonds were issued by your state or a municipality within your state.

Just as you can buy mutual funds that hold a large number of stocks, you can buy bond funds that are professionally managed. Some of these funds are set up to be state specific which allows you to invest in a fund for your home state. This gives you the ability to have exempt income for both federal and state purposes. These funds are convenient for those who do not want to buy their own diversified portfolio of bonds.

Effect on Alternative Minimum Tax

Interest earned on municipal bonds that are labeled "private activity" bonds is exempt from regular federal income tax but is subject to the alternative minimum tax.

Effect on Taxation of Social Security

Those who receive Social Security benefits find that a portion of those benefits may be subject to federal income tax. The higher the recipient's income is, the more of his or her benefits are taxable, up to a maximum of 85 percent of those benefits.

Even though interest earned on municipal bonds is not subject to federal income tax, that interest is added to other income in determining how much of the bondholders' Social Security benefits are taxable.

Deducting Interest Expense

Generally, expenses incurred to earn taxable income are deductible, with certain limitations. However, expenses incurred to earn tax-exempt income are not deductible. Therefore, if you borrow funds to invest in municipal bonds, the interest you pay on the borrowed funds will not be deductible.

Risk

The default risk is relatively low with municipal bonds, since they are issued by government agencies, and are usually insured as well. However, there is another risk that must be carefully considered. That is the market risk, which means that the market value of your bond may move up or down as the current interest rate changes.

The rate paid by a bond you own will not change during the life of that bond, but the rates paid by newly issued bonds will change from time to time. If market interest rates go up, the resale value of your bond will decrease. If you tried to sell your bond, a buyer would pay only a discounted price since your bond pays interest at a rate lower than that of newly issued bonds. On the other hand, if market interest rates drop, the value of your bond will rise.

The longer the remaining term is on your bond, the

more the value will move in response to the changing of current interest rates. Of course, if you hold your bond to full term, you will receive the par value of the bond upon redemption. So this change in market value really affects you only if you sell the bond before it matures.

The value of bonds may also move inversely with the stock market. When the stock market performs poorly, disappointed investors put more of their money into bonds. That additional demand may move the value of bonds upward. The opposite can be true as well when the stock market rallies.

Capital Gains and Losses

If you sell a municipal bond before it matures, any gain or loss you realize will be taxable or deductible under the same rules that apply to sales of stocks.

Premiums and Discounts

If you purchase a bond at a premium, because it pays a favorable interest rate, that premium is amortized (written off) over the remaining term of the bond. There is no deduction available for the amortized premium, but it reduces your basis in the bond. The basis affects the gain or loss you might incur if you resell the bond before maturity.

If you buy a bond with a market discount, that discount is accreted into income over the remaining term. That accretion is considered to be additional tax-exempt income.

United States Savings Bonds

Another reliable investment is the U.S. Savings Bond.

I Bonds and EE Bonds accrue interest monthly at variable rates and the interest compounds semi-annually. Interest earned on these bonds is not paid, and is not subject to federal income tax, until the bonds are redeemed. If used for qualified higher education expenses, earnings may be exempt from federal income taxes.

The interest earned on savings bonds is exempt from state and local income taxes.

An important consideration for any investment is liquidity. Savings bonds can be cashed in any time after a year from the date of purchase. There is no commission or fee to buy or to redeem savings bonds. However, if you redeem a savings bond within five years after buying it, you lose the last three months of earned interest.

Savings bonds are about as close to being risk-free as any investment can get since they are backed by the United States Treasury. If lost, stolen, or destroyed, they can be replaced without charge.

Savings bonds can be purchased in small denominations, and are readily available at local banks. Some employers offer payroll savings plans which systematically acquire bonds for employees. You can also buy bonds on-line directly from the U.S. Treasury by using a credit card.

Visit *www.USBonds.gov* and *www.InvestingInBonds.com* for more information.

Conclusion

Some investors consider bonds to be too lame and tame, but bonds sure do look good when the stock market drops. Since there is a tendency for the stock market and the bond market to move inversely, bonds can help investors diversify. Every investor should consider government bonds as a way to earn tax-free or tax deferred income, and to diversify his or her portfolio.

Tax Deferred Annuities

Any investor who wants to postpone taxes on investment income—that's you—needs to know about tax deferred annuities. Large amounts can be put into an annuity, and invested in a variety of diversified securities, including bond and stock funds. The earnings are not subject to income taxes until distributed to the owner. And, unlike IRAs, nonqualified annuities do not have to begin distributions when the owners reach a certain age.

Contributions to the Annuity

For tax purposes, the amount of contributions that can be put into an annuity is virtually unlimited. So you can use a single premium contract to quickly invest a large amount, by making only one or a few contributions.

Or you can obtain an installment premium contract and put in a series of contributions, which can be flexible or scheduled. Flexible premium contracts allow you to contribute as much as you wish at any time, within specified limits. Scheduled premium contracts specify the amount and frequency of contributions.

Earnings

Fixed annuity contracts generate income at an interest rate set by the company that issues the contract.

Variable annuity contracts allow you to invest your contributions in one or more mutual funds. As a result, the value of a variable annuity fluctuates with the performance of those mutual funds.

Some variable annuities have features that enable you to lock in a minimum return and a minimum distribution regardless of whether your investment accounts performed well.

Since annuity contracts are (by IRS regulations) considered to be a life insurance product, they also offer a death benefit. This is payable to the beneficiary if the annuitant (owner) dies prior to or during the distribution. This death benefit can also be locked in to the higher of the cash value or the fund balance over a specified period of time. This allows the earnings to be locked in even if the cash value of the account at the time of death is less than the initial deposit.

Most good annuities also offer some other type of principal protection benefit to protect against a loss of the principal. These features do come at an additional charge, but are usually worthwhile, especially in a volatile market.

Distributions

Annuity contracts can be either "deferred" or "immediate." In a deferred annuity, distributions are deferred until some future date. With an immediate annuity, the annuitant begins receiving periodic distributions right after his first contribution to the contract.

Because contributions to annuities are non-deductible, distributions of the amounts contributed are not taxable. However, any earnings in the annuity are taxable upon distribution. Unfortunately, a complex set of rules are used to determine how much of a distribution is considered to be a return of the owner's contributions and how much is taxable earnings.

Distributions can be received on a one-time or sporadic basis. Or, the owner can choose to annuitize the contract, meaning that distributions will be made either for life or periodically over a term certain, such as ten or twenty years. To reduce their risk, some owners prefer for distributions to continue for their lifetime or a term certain, whichever is longer. Of course, the longer the distribution period, the smaller each distribution will be. The "life only" option often pays the highest distribution per payment, so those who don't need to leave money to a beneficiary usually elect this option.

If a lump-sum distribution is received, the earnings in the contract are considered to come out first. This means that the lump-sum distribution is fully taxable to the extent of untaxed earnings in the annuity. But, if the owner annuitizes, a portion of each distribution is treated as a tax-free return of contributions and the rest of each distribution is considered to be taxable earnings.

The non-taxable portion of each distribution is determined by the exclusion ratio, which is the investment in the contract divided by the expected return on the contract.

"Investment in the contract" is defined under Internal Revenue Code (IRC) section 72 as your total contributions, less any prior distributions that were not taxable.

The expected return is calculated by multiplying the total annual annuity payment by an expected return multiple that can be based on your life expectancy or a fixed number of years stated in the contract. The exclusion ratio applies until your investment in the contract has been recovered. After recovery of your full investment in the contract, the entire distribution will be taxed as ordinary income.

All this means is that a portion of each distribution is treated as a non-taxable return of your contributions. And the rest of the distribution is considered to be from the annuity's earnings, which are taxable. But most people choose to receive a lump-sum distribution from the annuity, rather than actually annuitizing it anyway.

If you receive a distribution before you reach age 59 ½, you may have to pay Uncle Sam a ten percent penalty on the taxable portion, in addition to the income tax. I hate it when that happens.

But most annuity contracts allow a distribution of up to ten percent of the cash value without surrender charges to help owners access some of the funds when needed. This would still be subject to ordinary income taxes, and perhaps the ten percent penalty.

Exchanges

A taxable event arises when an annuity contract is surrendered or matures. However, IRC Section 1035 permits certain exchanges of annuity contracts to be tax-free. To qualify, the exchange has to be 1) a life insurance contract for an annuity contract; 2) an endowment contract for an annuity contract; or 3) an annuity contract for another annuity contract.

One appealing option is to use the cash value in a life insurance contract as a payment towards a deferred or immediate annuity. This is sometimes called "modern security." It is simply converting the equity in a life policy into a stream of income. This can be a great tool for seniors who want to increase their spendable income and no longer need much life insurance.

Expenses

It is important to understand the costs associated with annuity contracts. The most common costs are:

Contract charge—This is a flat fee charged by the issuing company to administer and maintain your contract.

Fund expense—This charge is paid to the mutual funds for managing the investments.

Insurance charge—This is commonly associated with variable annuity contracts that provide a minimum death benefit upon your premature death.

Surrender charge—This generally applies to contracts that are terminated by the owner during the early contract years. Its purpose is to provide the issuing company some assurance that the funds will be available to them for at least a certain number of years by discouraging you from canceling your contract prematurely.

But Consider This

Earnings in annuities are taxed as ordinary income upon distribution. Therefore, dividends and capital gains within annuities do not qualify for the lower federal tax rates normally available for dividends and long-term capital gains (maximum 15%). But then again, that low rate on those two types of income is schedule to end after 2008, and annuities are best suited for long-term investing.

Conclusion

Tax deferred annuities may fit your long-term financial plan by offering tax deferred compounding, investment diversification, and substantial savings for retirement. There are many variations on tax deferred annuity contracts. Consult your investment advisor and compare contract prospectuses from different companies before investing.

The Roth IRA

The Roth IRA allows invested funds to grow tax-free. Although contributions to a Roth IRA are not deductible, if you play by the rules, you will never have to pay tax on any of the Roth's earnings.

Contributions

You can contribute up to $3,000 to a Roth IRA in 2004. In 2005, the annual maximum increases to $4,000. The limit will increase to $5,000 in 2008, with additional increases of $500 each following year (unless Congress monkeys with it). Those over age 50 can make an additional $500 catch-up contribution (for 2004 and for 2005). The annual catch-up contribution limit will increase to $1,000 after 2005.

Not everyone is allowed to make contributions, however. First, you must have *earned* income (as opposed to investment income) at least equal to the amount contributed to the Roth.

Second, if your adjusted gross income (AGI) exceeds a certain limit, you are not eligible to make Roth IRA contributions. These limitations are determined by your filing status. If you are single, your maximum allowed contribution will begin to phase out once your AGI exceeds $95,000. Once your AGI is over $110,000, no contribution can be made to a Roth IRA.

If you are married filing jointly, the maximum contribution (per spouse) is phased out once your AGI hits $150,000 and eliminated at $160,000. (If married but filing separately, your allowable contribution is eliminated once your AGI reaches just $10,000. Yikes!) None of these numbers are currently set to be adjusted for inflation.

The maximum contribution allowance is also reduced by any contribution to a traditional IRA. But contributions can be made to a Roth IRA even if you are a participant in a qualified plan, such as a 401(k), 403(b), or profit-sharing plan.

An advantage of Roth IRAs over traditional IRAs is that you are not forced to stop contributing to a Roth IRA at the age of 70 ½. Another advantage with a Roth is that there are no minimum distribution requirements once you reach the age of 70 ½. This can be an excellent tool for estate planning purposes.

Rollovers

You may prefer the tax-*free* earnings potential of the Roth IRA over the tax-*deferred* benefits of your traditional IRA. If so, it may be worthwhile to convert your traditional IRA to a Roth IRA.

You can convert to a Roth IRA if your AGI (with a few modifications) does not exceed $100,000 this year. The amount that you convert will be taxed to you this year because it has never been included in your taxable income. But you will not have to pay the 10% early withdrawal penalty, unless you withdraw part of the converted amount within the five-year period following the conversion.

A conversion will be most profitable to you if you have a

long time before you expect to withdraw the earnings, are currently in a relatively low tax bracket, and have cash available to pay income taxes that will be created by the conversion.

Distributions

Qualified distributions from a Roth IRA are not taxed. The most important aspect to determining whether a distribution is qualified is the timing of the distribution. Since a Roth IRA is a retirement account, you generally must have reached the age of 59 ½ before the distributions qualify. But there are three exceptions to this rule.

First, you can receive up to $10,000 of distributions to help purchase your first home. Second, you can take qualified distributions if you become disabled. Finally, beneficiaries can take distributions from a Roth IRA following the owner's death.

For *any* distribution to be considered a qualified distribution, it must take place after a 5-tax year holding period. In other words, you must wait at least five tax years following the year in which you made the *initial* contribution to the Roth.

If you take a nonqualified distribution from a Roth IRA, it will be treated as a return of capital to the extent of your contributions. (Since you have already paid taxes on any amount contributed to the Roth, this portion of the distribution is non-taxable.) Any nonqualified distribution that exceeds your contributions is included in your taxable income.

The 10% Penalty

If the 5-tax year holding period is not met, the taxable portion of a nonqualified distribution is subject to a 10% penalty (as well as income tax) unless the owner is 59 ½ years old, disabled or deceased.

Conclusion

Roth IRAs are one of the most popular retirement vehicles because they provide tax-free compounding and a wide variety of investment choices. For an illustration of the importance of tax-free compounding, see The Power of Tax-Free Compounding found earlier in this book. If you are eligible to make Roth IRA contributions, do it.

Investing for Education

Free tuition! Get paid to attend college! Okay, not really. But, there are some great ways to keep up with the spiraling costs of higher education.

Coverdell Education Savings Accounts

Coverdell education savings accounts (ESAs) can be used to accumulate funds that will later pay for educational expenses. Contributions to ESAs are not deductible, but the investment grows tax-free. If the funds are withdrawn to pay for higher education expenses, the appreciation in value is never taxed.

Contributions to ESAs can be up to $2,000 per child each year. Note that the $2,000 limit is per beneficiary, not per contributor. You may make contributions for one year as late as April 15 of the following year.

Financial institutions and brokerage firms offer a wide variety of investment options for funds in ESAs.

Funds can be withdrawn tax-free to pay for elementary and secondary school tuition, as well as for college expenses. Corporations and other entities (including tax-exempt organizations) are permitted to make non-deductible contributions to ESAs.

To be eligible to make a contribution, an individual's

income must be below certain levels. The contribution amount phases out for singles with modified adjusted gross income between $95,000 and $110,000, and between $190,000 and $220,000 for married couples. You may be able to circumvent this income limit by gifting cash to a grandparent or to the child (or the child's guardian), who would then decide to make a contribution to the child's ESA.

A gift to a minor may legally be considered to be a gift to the minor's guardian. Check with your attorney about whether such a gift would be considered to be a gift of a future interest, which may not be eligible for the annual gift tax exclusion.

Qualified Tuition Programs (Section 529 Plans)

Qualified tuition programs, also known as Section 529 plans, help parents save for higher education expenses while avoiding income tax and reducing the parents' taxable estates.

There are two types of plans: college savings accounts and prepaid tuition programs.

College savings accounts are generally more flexible and even allow the contributor to take the money back from the plan. This is one of the very few ways to get money out of your estate while keeping strings attached. However, a 10-percent penalty and income taxes on the earnings apply if the amount withdrawn is not used to pay for higher education expenses.

If you choose to go with a prepaid tuition program, be sure the funds will be transferable if the beneficiary does not attend college. Individuals are allowed to purchase tuition credits or certificates only on behalf of a designated beneficiary.

The 529 plans are more attractive than ESAs to individuals with higher incomes because the contribution limits for 529 plans are not based on the contributor's income.

Parents may gift up to $55,000 ($110,000 if married filing jointly) per child in a single tax year. The $55,000 gift is coordinated with the gift tax annual exclusion to avoid the gift tax. The parent can choose to treat the gift as though one-fifth of the total was given in each of 5 years. Therefore, to completely exclude the funds from the parent's taxable estate, the parent may have to live 5 years after making the gift. Gift tax returns must be filed.

Grandparents and rich friends can also set up a 529 plan. These plans allow grandparents to reduce their taxable estates without gift tax, while funding education for their grandchildren.

As with ESAs, contributions to 529 plans are not deductible for federal income tax purposes. Some states allow deductions for state income tax purposes. But if the beneficiary does not attend college in that state, you may have to fork over the state tax savings.

The funds inside these plans can be invested in a variety of choices, usually including mutual funds and bond funds. The income earned within the plan is withdrawn tax-free if the funds are used for qualified higher education expenses.

The exclusion from gross income for distributions from a prepaid tuition program, which is established and maintained by an entity other than a state, is effective for taxable years beginning after 2003.

There are many variations of 529 plans and all programs are not created equally. Investigate different plans before you decide.

Conclusion

Your children and grandchildren asked me to encourage you to prepare for their education expenses now. So, take advantage of these plans that offer tax-free compounding of your dollars.

412(I) Plans

Traditional retirement plans do not allow large enough contributions for some established small business owners and professionals. This is especially true for those who are nearing retirement but have fallen behind in saving for retirement. Many small business owners have poured all of their profits back into their businesses instead of into retirement plans. Others may wish to make contributions that exceed the $40,000 limit on deductible contributions to other retirement plans. A section 412(i) plan may be just the right plan for these individuals to set aside large amounts for retirement in the near future.

A section 412(i) plan typically guarantees future benefits based on annuity and insurance contracts. Because the benefits are fully insured, the plans are very conservative from an investment standpoint.

Who would Benefit?

Section 412(i) plans are not the best retirement plans for everyone. However, certain circumstances make these plans ideal for some business owners. These plans are particularly attractive to business owners and self-employed individuals who:

Have fewer than 5 employees,

Are over the age of 40,

Want to significantly increase current tax deductions for contributions to a plan,

Have stable cash flow, and

Want investments to be put into stable assets.

Advantages

There are several advantages to 412(i) plans. First, they are inexpensive to set up and maintain. The reason for this is that the plans do not require expensive actuarial computations as in other defined benefit plans because these plans are funded with insurance and annuity products. This type of plan costs only a few hundred dollars to set up. The plans are less expensive to maintain than other types of plans, because there are no IRS filing requirements.

Another benefit of these plans is that they produce a guaranteed retirement benefit. Because future benefits are derived from annuity contracts, it is possible to determine the exact amount of monthly retirement benefits that the plan will generate. A fully funded plan can produce retirement income of as much as $165,000 per year under current rules. These plans also produce a significant death benefit in the event of the individual's death before retirement depending on the amount of life insurance included in the plan.

As an individual nears retirement, a 412(i) plan can provide deductions for contributions that are far larger than other types of plan. Up to $350,000 can be deducted depending on the age of the employee. The annual contributions are greatest during the first few years of the plan. The amount to contribute declines each year as the plan becomes funded.

Another advantage to 412(i) plans is that they are much easier on the company that establishes the plan. The company will not show a liability on its books. A company will not have over or under-funding issues, as with other types of defined benefit plans, with this type of plan because the plan is funded on an annual basis. The annual funding is merely the amount of premiums for the life insurance and annuities in the plan. Over and under-funding can produce negative results in penalties and extra taxes.

The company can pay into plans on an annual basis instead of quarterly.

Disadvantages

Although 412(i) plans are a great tool, there are a few drawbacks. There may be a larger initial set-up cost compared to noninsured plans. However, as stated before, the maintenance costs usually are below other plans costs. There is no flexibility in the choice of investments for the plan. The plans also cannot be borrowed against. Section 412(i) plans must also be nondiscriminatory. For this reason the plan does not work well for companies that have more than a few rank and file employees. The plans are also more conservative, which means there is less growth potential.

Another potential problem with 412(i) plans is that the IRS has vowed to crack down on abusive plans. Because of this, it is essential for the plans to follow certain guidelines which distinguish an acceptable 412(i) plan from an abusive plan. To be acceptable the plan should be primarily for the purpose of retirement not insurance. An acceptable plan should have less than 25% of the total cost attributable to life insurance premiums. They also must be permanent; they should not be set up to take large deductions for the first few years only to be rolled over into a different plan once the deductible contributions start decreasing.

Conclusion

A 412(i) plan can provide significant tax and retirement benefits to small business owners and professionals who qualify. The plan offers large tax deductions as well as predictable benefits upon retirement.

Owners Only 401(k)

Do you own your own business or receive self-employment income? Are you interested in maximizing your retirement savings? If so, the Owners Only 401(k) Plan, sometimes referred to as an "owner (k) plan", is a highly-effective retirement planning option that you should consider.

The Owners Only 401(k) Plan is suitable for any type of business (sole proprietorship, partnership, corporation or limited liability company) whose only employees are the business owner(s) and the owner's immediate family members.

An owner k plan is a special type of 401(k) plan set up specifically for small businesses that employ only the owner and his or her family members. A common misperception of owner k plans is that they are only for sole proprietors. This is not the case. Any type of business including a sole proprietorship, partnership, corporation or limited liability company is eligible provided that the only eligible employees are the business owner(s) and the owners' immediate family members. An eligible company can also have part-time employees, or employees under 21, but these employees can not work over 1,000 hours a year, excluding the spouse.

The contributions allowed with this plan include:

Employee's elective deferrals: Each employee can contribute up to $13,000 (2004) or 100% of his/her eligible compensation.

Profit sharing contribution: An employer corporation can contribute up to 25% of each employee's compensation. The limits for a sole-proprietorship are based on modified net profit and will be equal to 20% of this number.

Catch-up contributions: A catch-up contribution can be made for an employee who has reached the age of 50 prior to yearend. These additional contributions can be made for a maximum of $3,000 (2004). The maximum deferral is increased for these contributions thus the total amount deferred can be in excess of the maximum deferral amounts as discussed below.

As with other plans, contributions to an Owners Only 401(k) plan are tax deductible and the earnings grow tax-deferred. If you and your spouse co-own a business, this gives the two of you the potential to put aside for retirement up to $82,000 per year, plus any catch-up contributions.

Contribution Limits

The following is a breakdown, at various compensation levels, of the maximum deductible contributions for each type of retirement plan for the 2004 calendar year.

Earnings	Owners Only 401(k)	Profit Sharing Only	SEP	SIMPLE IRA
$25,000	$19,250	$6,250	$6,250	$9,750
$50,000	$25,500	$12,500	$12,500	$10,500
$100,000	$38,000	$25,000	$25,000	$12,000

The maximum total deferral is equal to $41,000 per person (for 2004) before taking into consideration any catch-up contributions for employees 50 and older. As you can see, contributions to an Owners Only 401(k) plan far exceed the limits that apply to a SEP IRA, SIMPLE IRA, or profit-sharing plan.

Example

Linda, age 55, owns a profitable corporation. How much can she defer if the corporation pays her $100,000 as W-2 wages in 2004?

The profit sharing contribution can be $25,000 (25% of $100,000).

Her salary deferral can be $13,000.

The catch-up contribution (for age 50+) can be $3,000.

This results in a total deferral for the year of $41,000.

Additional Benefits

This plan allows your contributions to be flexible from year to year. Since the plan is based on a profit sharing plan concept, the owner can make contributions at his/her discretion. If company earnings are lower one year, the contribution can be reduced or eliminated altogether based on business needs. In addition, there is a wide variety of investment options available, allowing diversification.

As with traditional 401(k) plans, you can borrow from your account in the Owners Only 401(k) plan, up to the greater of $50,000 or 50% of the account balance. This provides immediate access to cash when needed, but this option should not be used unless absolutely necessary. As with loans from traditional 401(k) plans, if you don't repay the loan, the outstanding balance will be considered a distribution. The distribution will be subject to income tax and, unless an exception is met, a 10% penalty.

Another benefit is that most plans have the ability to accept transfer of other retirement plan assets including profit sharing and money-purchase plans, traditional IRA's and SEP IRA's into your 401(k).

Protecting Your Savings

This plan may also provide some legal protection for your retirement savings if there are at least two participants. Assets within this plan (and other qualified plans) may be inaccessible to a plaintiff targeting you or your business with a predatory lawsuit. In contrast, IRA funds may be completely vulnerable. When setting up an Owners Only 401(k) plan, you may want to consider designing the plan to allow rollovers into the plan. Then, perhaps you could help protect your IRA funds by rolling them into the 401(k). Consult your attorney for more information.

The Costs

Another advantage of the Owners Only 401(k) plan is the fact that it is a relatively easy and low cost plan to establish and maintain. The annual administrative cost of managing the plan may be as little as $150 to $200. This low cost is partly due to the plan being free of the infamous nondiscrimination testing that normally applies to Section 401(k) plans. This allows the Owners Only 401(k) plan to be drafted and administered much more simply and cost effectively than for other qualified plans. Also, if the plan has less than $100,000 in assets, a Form 5500 annual report does not have to be filed with the IRS; otherwise the costs for this filing will need to be considered.

Conclusion

The Owners Only 401(k) helps qualifying workers and their spouses maximize and protect their retirement savings with little administrative costs. The flexibility of these plans as well as the ability to contribute large amounts can make this a superior plan for a small business owner.

Private Pensions

Are you looking for a way to invest some money so it can grow tax free, and the funds can be withdrawn without penalty and withdrawal fees? If so, and if you want additional life insurance, the private pension may be just for you.

The private pension is not really a pension plan, but is a life insurance policy that, due to the way the IRS looks at the policy, allows it to grow and maximizes the tax-free accumulation of funds. It is a very flexible life insurance vehicle that has many benefits.

The Tax Benefits

Life insurance policies can be structured to offer great tax savings. First, they can allow tax-free cash value accumulation. This is accomplished through flexible contribution schedules, which determine the amounts and the timing of future withdrawals. Insurance companies offer access to a wide variety of investment options and interest rates for the cash value of a policy.

The second tax advantage is the death benefit, which can be received by the beneficiaries free of income tax. The death benefit can be received free of estate tax also, if set up properly.

Certain life insurance policies also offer major tax advantages when it comes to withdrawing funds from the policies. You can withdraw, without tax, the amount you previously paid in. In addition, after making contributions for a few years, you can borrow the earnings that have accumulated in your policy over those years. In essence, you are accessing the investments' growth tax—free. Many policies will allow you to adjust the death benefit if more or less insurance is desired and your cash flow needs change. At your death, the death benefit is netted against (reduced by) the withdrawals and borrowings, and any remaining death benefit goes to the policy's beneficiaries.

This means that you can put cash into the policy where it is invested and grows tax-free. Later, perhaps during retirement, you withdraw the funds you put in without triggering tax. You can also borrow the tax-free earnings that have accumulated. Interest will accrue on the loan, but you never have to actually repay the loan or pay the accrued interest. Following your death, the beneficiaries of the policy simply receive the death benefit, less the withdrawals, the loan balance, and the accrued interest.

Maximizing the Tax-Free Growth

Some insurance companies have carefully designed policies to *maximize* the tax-free earning potential of these particular policies and to *minimize* the death benefit. These policies are specifically designed for those who want to take advantage of the tax-free earning potential but are not really in need of additional life insurance. They go as far to minimize the death benefit as they can, without falling outside of the Internal Revenue Code's requirements for a life insurance policy.

These policies are known by various names, such as "private pensions," "life insurance retirement programs," "supplemental life insurance plans," and "deferred compensation plans." These plans have existed for more than twenty years. They are also commonly used in business settings for employee retention and recruiting purposes.

How They Qualify

To qualify for these tax benefits, the policy has to avoid being classified as a modified endowment contract (MEC). The purpose of the MEC rules is to prevent life insurance from being used as a short-term investment.

So, the policy must meet two requirements. First, it must meet the 7-pay test. Second, it cannot be a policy you received in exchange for one that was a MEC. If there is any material change in a policy, it will be required to meet the 7-pay test again.

In order to meet the 7-pay test, the "net level premium" per year must not be exceeded for the first seven years. (This requirement prevents frontloading the policy, the way many people did with single-premium policies back in the 1980s.) However, this may be avoided using a variable death benefit, which allows you to increase the death benefit in years when contributions are being made and to reduce the death benefit when withdrawals begin.

The net level premium is an amount determined by the Internal Revenue Code. Your policy could fail the 7-pay test if one year's contribution is greater than the net level premium.

Although there is really no limit on the total amount that can be invested, they are usually set up with contributions scheduled for 15 years. However, there is great flexibility in creating the contribution schedule, depending on the desired amounts and timing of withdrawals.

Timing

Timing is always important in tax planning. The timing of contributions, withdrawals, and loans must be well planned. The policy can be structured for withdrawals of a particular amount per year for a number of years, or it can be designed for the maximum withdrawals based on a certain premium payment. Another alternative is to set the premium payments and the withdrawals at certain levels in order to adjust the death benefit over the lifetime of the policy to fit your needs.

These policies are often designed to fill the gaps between retirement and the availability of other retirement funds. Many plan for withdrawals between retirement and reaching age 59 1/2, when 401(k) funds may be withdrawn without penalty. Others plan their withdrawals for the years before Social Security benefits are available.

The policy must not be allowed to lapse. If the policy lapses, you may be immediately taxed on some or all of the loans taken out on the policy.

Conclusion

Many insurance companies use strategies based on these rules to set up "private pension" plans. These polices are well worth considering if you need another avenue for tax-free, long-term investing and want some additional life insurance. Because of the time limits on tax-free withdrawals, the earlier you start, the better.

Selling Assets Through A VUL

Creative planners sometimes use a variable universal life (VUL) insurance policy to acquire an appreciated asset from the insured, and then have the policy sell that asset. This strategy takes advantage of a life insurance policy's ability to buy and sell investments without paying taxes on the gains.

How does it Work?

Suppose you want to sell some highly appreciated stock. But, of course, you prefer to defer capital gains tax on that sale. So, you buy a VUL policy on your own life. The VUL buys the stock from you at the stock's fair market value. The VUL later sells the stock to a third party without taxation.

To pay you for the stock, the VUL may issue you a private annuity. You are required to recognize gain from the stock sale as you receive payments under the private annuity. This spreads the gain recognition over your entire lifetime. (Please see the chapter on Private Annuities for more details.)

Example

If you own the stock of an S corporation, here is how you might apply this strategy to sell your stock. First, you need to transfer the stock to an electing small business trust (ESBT) in exchange for a private annuity. An ESBT is one of the very few types of entities permitted to own S corporation stock.

The ESBT needs to have a primary and a secondary beneficiary, but the beneficiary may be expected to get little or no money from the trust. The beneficiary could be a charity of your choice or your children. You would no longer be allowed to personally run the S corporation directly. You need to appoint a bank or the company that set the trust up to serve as the trustee for the ESBT.

The next step is for the ESBT to liquidate the S corporation and put the business assets into a newly formed limited liability company (LLC). The purpose of this step is to get the business into a type of entity that can be owned by a life insurance policy. Since the ESBT paid fair market value for the S corporation stock, there should be little or no tax upon liquidation of the S corporation.

You then need to purchase a variable universal life insurance policy. The policy then buys the LLC from the ESBT. (Since the trust will have just bought the business at its fair market value, and will promptly sell it at fair market value, there should be little or no taxable gain or loss on this sale.) A promissory note could be issued by the VUL policy to the ESBT equal in amount to the value of the business. But the VUL won't have enough cash to fund payments to the ESBT. So, at this point, the VUL policy may assume the ESBT's obligation to you under the private annuity in satisfaction of the VUL's note payable to the ESBT. That obligation should result in the trust having little or no net value. The ESBT may then have some cash, but no securities, insurance or other assets.

When the VUL policy acquires the LLC, the consideration given is the VUL's assumption of the private annuity obligation, and some cash (perhaps $20,000). The VUL policy will then owe the private annuity to you.

At this point, you own the VUL policy, which owns the LLC, which owns the operating assets of your former S corporation.

It is very important to see that you relinquish control of the business to the trustee when you transfer the stock to the ESBT. The trustee that you chose will then have control. When the business is acquired by the VUL policy (which may occur the next day) you may have more control (since you own the VUL policy). But even after the business is acquired by the VUL policy, it is recommended that you not directly handle daily transactions of the business, such as signing checks.

If the business generates profits after this, those profits are reported to the VUL policy, which pays no income tax. When an acceptable offer is received for the business, the VUL may be able to sell it without a taxable gain since life insurance policies are permitted to buy and sell securities without taxation.

Once your business has been sold, the VUL policy can reinvest the proceeds which grow tax-free inside the policy.

The asset protection aspect of this is centered on state laws that may protect life insurance policies from claims of creditors. So, if you are the target of a predatory lawsuit, a large portion of your wealth is owned by the VUL policy that may be protected from creditors by state law.

You may be able to borrow from the policy, to get cash into your hands. Current law does not require that these loans be repaid until death. The total loan balance, including accrued interest, would simply be offset against the death proceeds.

Following your death, the VUL policy would pay the death benefit, net of the loan balance, to the beneficiaries. Because it will be a variable policy, the total death benefit is to include whatever amount the policy's assets have grown to at that point. In other words, the death benefit is to be whatever investments are in the policy, plus the policy's death benefit, which may be substantial.

The Particulars

Although insurance companies commonly issue VULs, most severely limit the types of investments that can be held inside them. South Carolina and some foreign jurisdictions have approved policies that allow for this type of transaction.

Be sure that the policy's investments meet the diversification requirements.

Conclusion

Selling an appreciated asset through a VUL is a complicated process, but may result in substantial tax savings to anyone who does it correctly.

Life Insurance Trusts

Many Americans are not aware that the estates they are building could be large enough to be subject to the estate tax. However, many estates are taxable because those estates include life insurance proceeds.

It is well known that life insurance proceeds are not subject to *income* tax. However, your life insurance proceeds may be subject to estate tax if your estate receives (or benefits from) those proceeds. Also, the proceeds may be subject to estate tax if you possessed any incidents of ownership in the policy within three years prior to death.

It would be disastrous for your life insurance proceeds to be subject to estate tax, since it means that the IRS could end up with half of those proceeds.

Using a Trust

If a life insurance policy is owned by an irrevocable trust, the proceeds can avoid the estate tax. The proceeds may avoid probate as well, allowing the cash to get to your heirs much more quickly.

An irrevocable life insurance trust (ILIT) is typically created by establishing a standard irrevocable trust. An attorney is needed to draft the documents, which name the trustee and beneficiaries. The insured then periodically puts cash into the trust to pay the policy's premiums.

If you transfer an existing policy to the trust, the transfer must take place more than three years prior to your death for the estate tax to be avoided. Therefore, it is better for the trust to own the policy as soon as the policy is issued.

Paying the Premiums

When you put money into the ILIT to pay the premiums, that cash is considered to be a gift to the trust's beneficiaries. If structured properly, the gift will qualify for the $11,000 annual exclusion. To the extent that the amount put in exceeds the annual exclusion of $11,000 per recipient, the gift tax may initially be offset by your unified credit. Once the unified credit has been fully utilized, cash contributions to the trust for the premium payments may create a gift tax. (The gift tax is essentially the same as the estate tax, but payment of the gift tax reduces the estate that will later be subject to estate tax.)

If and when the time comes that the premium payments will create a gift tax, you should explore creative ways to avoid that tax. For example, compensation arrangements between you and the beneficiaries could allow you to deduct payments made to them as compensation, and they could use the after-tax portion of that compensation to fund the policy's premium. It may also be possible for you to loan them the money needed to make the premium payment.

If you pay the trustee's fee, this payment would also be a gift to the trust's beneficiaries.

Before you Sign

It is important to structure the trust properly since it is irrevocable and you will not later have the opportunity to amend or revoke it. If you retain even the power to give instructions to the trustee, the IRS could require that the insurance proceeds be included in your taxable estate. If the inability to make changes concerns you, consider using a family limited partnership, instead of an ILIT, to own the policy.

Following your death, the trust would receive the policy's

death benefit. Once the trust receives the proceeds, those proceeds could be distributed to the trust's beneficiaries, who may put the cash into your estate in exchange for business interests or other property owned by your estate. This could work almost as if they were buying your property from your estate. The estate should not realize a gain on that sale subject to income tax since the basis in that property would have been stepped up to fair market value.

This type of trust could help your children avoid significant estate tax. It could also help provide them the liquidity they will need to protect their interests in your property. But once the policy is in the trust, you should not borrow from the policy.

If an existing policy is to be transferred into a trust, consider borrowing the cash surrender value before the transfer, or that cash surrender value will be considered a gift to the trust's beneficiaries.

Conclusion

A life insurance trust may be one of the easiest and least expensive ways for your family to avoid a substantial amount of estate tax. But remember that the trust must be irrevocable. If you later decide to cut off the beneficiaries, your only choice may be to stop funding the premiums. If you do stop, comparable life insurance coverage may not be available at that time to replace the terminated policy. But life insurance policies are intended to be tax-free. Be sure that half of your policy's death benefit isn't lost to estate tax.

Donating an Appreciated Asset

Internal Revenue Code Section 170 allows you to deduct donations made to recognized charities. If you donate money, the amount deductible is the amount you give, subject to certain limitations.

But there is a more effective way to donate to your favorite school, church or charity. This powerful tax-saving strategy is the donation of appreciated capital assets, such as stocks, bonds, art, collectibles or real estate.

You can deduct the fair market value of each donated asset as a charitable deduction on your tax return. Here's the big benefit: The appreciation of those assets is never reported as income or gain on your tax return. So, before you pull out your checkbook, take a look at your portfolio and other property.

You can donate stock by simply asking your broker to transfer it to the charity's account. The charity, which is exempt from capital gain taxes, can sell the stock as needed.

Example

Let's say you donate 100 shares of stock to a charity. You paid $2,000 for those shares about five years ago. The shares are worth $6,500 on the date of your donation. You can claim a $6,500 charitable deduction and never pay capital gains tax on the $4,500 of appreciation.

The Details

There are some important points to remember. To deduct the fair market value, you must have owned the asset longer than a year before you donate it. A year and a day is enough.

Deductions for non-cash charitable donations can offset only thirty percent of an individual taxpayer's adjusted gross income for any one tax year. Any amount in excess of this limit may be carried forward and deducted the next year, subject to that same income limit in that year. You can carry it forward up to five years, if necessary, to get your full deduction.

Corporations may take advantage of this benefit as well, but corporations can deduct charitable contributions of up to only ten percent of their taxable income each year. They get to carry forward excess deductions up to five years.

S corporations and partnerships (including LLCs taxed as partnerships) can use this tax advantage as well. The charitable deduction flows through to the owners.

An appraisal is required for a contribution of an asset (other than publicly traded stock) with a fair market value of more than $5,000. The cost of the appraisal may be claimed as a miscellaneous itemized deduction. Related expenses, such as mileage (14 cents per mile) may be deductible also.

Be sure to get and keep a written acknowledgement from the charity.

Conclusion

The next time you're feeling generous, remember that donating an appreciated capital asset can generate an immediate deduction and avoid capital gains tax.

Charitable Remainder Trusts

Enjoy paying capital gains taxes? I didn't think so. Perhaps you should consider using a charitable remainder trust, which is one of the most effective and popular tax strategies available.

The trust can be set up easily, and provides immediate tax benefits. You can transfer an asset into the trust and get a charitable contribution deduction on your income tax return for that year.

The amount of the deduction is the fair market value of the asset (if you have owned it for more than a year) discounted over the length of the trust. The length of the trust may be either a term certain or your lifetime. The longer the trust is expected to last, the lower your charitable contribution deduction will be. Many married couples choose to establish trusts that will last as long as either spouse is living.

The deduction for transfers of appreciated assets may offset only thirty percent of your adjusted gross income in any year. But, if the deduction is so large that you cannot use it all in one year, the unused portion can be carried forward for as many as five years.

The charitable remainder trust (CRT) is tax exempt and can therefore sell appreciated assets you put into it (including stock and real estate) without paying tax on the gains. This means that the full sale proceeds (not just the after-tax portion) can be invested, generating annual income for you for the rest of your life.

The proceeds received from selling the assets would be put into income-generating investments inside the CRT. Income would be distributed to you at least annually. You would have to pay income tax on the distributions as you receive them. However, your cash flow could be significantly more than it would be if you sold the appreciated assets yourself, paid tax on the gains, and then had only the after-tax sale proceeds to invest.

The CRT can distribute some of the principal to you as well. Depending on the distribution options you choose, you may be able to have up to 90% of the principal distributed back to you over your lifetime. But the less you leave for charity, the lower your charitable contribution deduction will be.

After your death, the remaining principal would go to the charity(ies) of your choice. If you are concerned about your heirs not getting the principal, you could use some of the income tax savings generated by your transfers to the CRT to purchase life insurance. At your death, your heirs would get the life insurance proceeds rather than the trust principal.

Some people use CRTs to avoid *ever* having to pay capital gains taxes. Rather than selling their appreciated stocks, for example, they transfer those stocks to the trust, which then sells them. They must be sure the property has been transferred to the CRT before a sale has been negotiated. Each transfer creates a current income tax deduction, and increases the subsequent income distributions to the contributor. (Is this a great exit strategy for a retiring business owner or what?)

This is also one of the few ways you can enjoy the income stream from investments for your lifetime without exposing those assets to the estate tax.

There are many variations available in setting up these trusts, but all CRTs are exempt from taxes (unless they have unrelated business income).

The amount distributed by the trust is based on a percentage rate, stipulated in the trust document, which cannot be less than five percent annually. The rate can be applied to the initial value of your contributions, or can be applied to the current value of the trust principal each year. The latter approach would result in distribution amounts fluctuating from year to year.

Example

A 55-year-old has owned stock since early in his career. The stock has a basis of $50,000 and a fair market value of $1 million. He wants to sell the stock and use the proceeds to fund an investment that will earn 6% annually.

First, let's look at what happens if he does not use a CRT. He sells the stock for $1,000,000, but then owes $185,000 in federal and state capital gain taxes. This leaves him with $815,000 to invest at 6%, which provides him annual income of $48,900. Following his death, his beneficiaries will get the principal of his investment, minus estate taxes.

Now let's look at what would happen if instead of selling the stock, he forms a CRT with income distributions to him for his remaining lifetime. (This example assumes that we are using an IRC section 7520 rate of 5.2 %.)

When he transfers his stock to the CRT, he can claim a charitable contribution deduction of $285,682. This deduction is calculated as the present value of $1 million at the end of his life expectancy as provided in IRS tables. This deduction saves him about $125,000 in federal and state income taxes (perhaps over a period of as many as six years).

The trust sells the stock tax-free for $1 million. The trust is then able to invest $1 million at 6%, which gives him annual income of $60,000.

The remaining principal in the trust goes to the charities of his choice upon his death rather than to his family. But his family gets the benefit of whatever he did with the $125,000 of income tax savings when he funded the trust. The family also benefits from the additional $11,100 of distributions he received annually (the difference between the $60,000 he received annually from the CRT and the $48,900 his investment would have earned if he had sold the stock without the CRT).

Note that he could have chosen a different distribution option and had the CRT distribute up to 90% of the principal to him. This would have given him a smaller tax deduction in the year of the donation, and the charity would have gotten much less following his death.

An Interesting Variation

Charitable lead trusts offer an interesting twist on the charitable trust. With this type of trust, it is the charity that receives the income during the trust term with the non-charitable beneficiaries receiving the remainder interest at the end of the trust term. The charitable remainder trust discussed earlier gives the benefit of the appreciation of assets to the charitable remainder beneficiary. On the other hand, charitable lead trusts result in the asset appreciation going to the non-charitable beneficiaries, or heirs. These can be very useful planning tools. A non-tax consideration for using this type of vehicle may be to postpone the transfer of assets to heirs that may not be ready or able to manage the assets appropriately.

To Know Before You Decide

Before signing any documents, be sure you understand all of the restrictions. For example, CRTs are irrevocable. This means you can't get the property back after putting it into the trust. You can, however, reserve the right to change charitable beneficiaries later if you want to.

Transferring passive activity property into a CRT does not free up suspended losses. Losses previously generated by that property remain suspended.

Also debt on the property, such as a mortgage, should not be transferred to the CRT. If property has debt on it, consider creative approaches, such as putting the property and debt into an LLC and then transferring your interest in the LLC to the trust.

Conclusion

Putting assets into a CRT entitles you to an immediate income tax deduction, allows you to receive income from the full sale proceeds, and avoids exposing your principal to estate tax. Strict guidelines must be followed to protect these tax benefits, so see Internal Revenue Code section 664. But, as the list of legitimate tax strategies grows shorter, the CRT will continue to grow in popularity.

Homeownership

Financial planners often advise their clients to buy the best house they can afford. This is because a house provides so many tax benefits as well as personal benefits, and may appreciate while you live in it. The appreciation may have a dramatic effect, since you can benefit from the leverage.

Your Home as a Tax-Free Investment

You are not required to pay income tax on the increase in the value of your home each year.

When you sell your home, all or some of the gain may not be taxable. For single individuals, up to $250,000 of gain is excludible from taxable income. For married couples filing a joint return, the excludible amount is $500,000.

Like any other tax break, certain requirements must be met. To qualify for the exclusion, you must have owned and used the home as your principal residence for at least two years out of the five years prior to the sale. To get the full $500,000 exclusion, both spouses must have used the house as their primary residence, but it is okay if it was owned by only one of the spouses.

You can claim this exclusion only every two years. For example, if you marry someone who has recently sold a home, you are not eligible for any exclusion until both spouses have met the two-year requirement for the next home to be sold. Furthermore, if you are using your home for business and have claimed depreciation deductions on that part of the home, you will be required to pay income tax on recent depreciation claimed on the home office.

If you have not lived in your home for two years, you may qualify for a smaller exclusion if the sale is caused by an employment change or health problems.

Please remember that your basis in your home may be well below the amount you paid for the home! This could have happened if you bought your home when the old tax rules were in effect. Under the old rules, you could defer recognition of gain on the sale of a principal residence by purchasing another residence. But, you had to reduce your basis in the new home by the amount of gain deferred on the sale of the old residence.

Also, when preparing to sell your residence, consider an opportunity for some tax-free income. If you spend a Saturday fixing up the house, you may be able sell the house for a little more. As long as you don't exceed the exclusion limit, the additional sales proceeds is really tax-free compensation for your day of labor.

Leverage

By borrowing to acquire your home, you have the opportunity to leverage your investment. Consider putting little of your own funds into the house, and borrowing the rest. Then when the property appreciates, you'll get a high return on the funds you put into it.

For example, if you have $20,000 of your funds in a $100,000 home, and its value appreciates by 10% one year, you've made a 50% tax deferred return on your $20,000.

If you had paid $100,000 of cash for the property, you would have made only a 10% return on a much larger amount of your money.

Also, asset protection attorneys often recommend keeping high levels of debt on homes. This strategy, known as equity-stripping, is designed to leave little equity for plaintiffs to target when they bring a predatory lawsuit against the owner. (Equity-stripping is one of the few strategies that will not cause the homeowner to lose favorable property tax status, such as the homestead exemption, or lose the capital gain exclusion upon later sale of the home.)

Interest on Acquisition Indebtedness

If you borrow to acquire or fix up your home, the mortgage interest expense on that "acquisition" indebtedness is tax-deductible. If you own a second personal residence, such as a vacation home, you can deduct interest related to acquiring or improving it as well.

As you would expect, the amount of deductible mortgage interest expense is limited. Interest is deductible for acquisition indebtedness up to $1,000,000. This amount can be divided between your first (principal) and second (vacation) home.

If you borrow more than $1,000,000, the interest you pay on the excess will not be deductible. However, interest paid on the portion of the debt that exceeds this limit may be deductible as investment interest expense, if your home or vacation home was purchased with appreciation in mind.

If you take out a second mortgage to improve your principal or vacation home, you will be allowed to deduct the interest if the total of your mortgages does not exceed the $1,000,000 limit.

If you refinance, and increase the amount of your debt, the interest you pay on the additional debt will not be considered to be interest on acquisition indebtedness. Interest you pay on that additional debt may be deductible, however, as interest on an equity loan.

Interest on Home Equity Loans

You can deduct interest paid on a home equity loan (or line of credit) of up to $100,000. Get this: interest paid on home equity debt is deductible even if the loan is used for personal purposes, such as a vacation. Home equity loans are a popular way of financing automobile purchases due to the deductibility of interest expense and low interest rates.

Property Taxes

Property taxes you pay on your homes are deductible in the year you pay them. Most mortgage servicing companies will pay property taxes out of escrowed funds by December

31 even though the payment may not be due until after the end of the year. Then, the borrower won't have to wait until the next year to get the deduction.

Conclusion

Your home is one of the most important financial investments you will make. It can provide you current deductions, tax deferred growth, and some tax-free gain when sold.

Since you can deduct interest on a total of $1,100,000, buy the best house you can afford and enjoy the deductions and appreciation.

Business Use of the Home

If you work out of an office in your home, you may be able to deduct home office expenses. But strict requirements must be met. First, the business part of your home must pass one of the "use" tests. Also, the area used for business must meet the "exclusive" and "regular" use requirements. In addition, those who are employees must meet the "convenience of the employer" requirement.

Use Tests

To deduct your home office expenses, you must first meet *any one* of the following three use tests:

1. Separate Structure

A separate, unattached structure on the same property as your home can qualify for business use of home deductions. This could be an unattached garage, studio, workshop, or office building.

2. Place to Meet Clients

You may meet the use test if you use your home office to meet or deal with clients in the normal course of your business. The clients must be physically present in your home office; telephone calls to them from your home office won't do the trick.

3. Principal Place of Business

There are two tests for determining whether your home office is your principal place of business. Your home office must satisfy *either* of these tests.

Management or administrative activities test: Your home office can qualify as your principal place of business if you use it regularly for administrative or management duties in your business. Administrative or management duties may include billing, bookkeeping, ordering supplies, and writing reports.

Relative importance / time test: For this test, there are two considerations in determining your principal place of business: (1) the *relative importance* of the activities you perform at each business location, and (2) the *amount of time* you spend at each business location.

Exclusive and Regular Use Requirements

In addition to meeting one of the use tests outlined above, your home office must be used *exclusively* and *regularly* in your business. The *exclusive use* requirement means that you must use your home office *only* for your business. The exclusive use test is strictly enforced by the Internal Revenue Service.

Regular use means that you use your home office in your business on a recurring basis. This generally means a few hours a week.

There's an exception to the exclusive and regular use requirements for storage space used by retailers or wholesalers.

"Convenience of the Employer" Requirement

An employee may deduct home office expenses only if the home office is maintained for the convenience of his or her employer.

Home Office Deductions

If use of your home office qualifies under the rules summarized above, you may deduct two sets of expenses.

Direct expenses benefit only the business part of your home. Examples are the costs of maintaining or repairing your office. Generally, 100% of direct expenses are deductible against business income.

Indirect expenses benefit both the business and personal areas of your home. Examples are mortgage interest, real estate taxes, as well as otherwise nondeductible expenses such as costs of a security system, utilities, insurance, and depreciation. Indirect expenses are deductible based on the percentage of your home used for business. The business-use percentage is usually determined by dividing the square footage of the office by the total square footage of the home.

Amount Limitations / Reporting Requirements

If gross income from the business use of your home equals or exceeds your total business expenses (including depreciation), you can deduct all of your business expenses related to the use of your home. However, if gross income from the business use of your home is less than your total business expenses, your deduction for certain expenses may be limited. Office deductions that are disallowed are carried forward to the next year. The calculation of the deduction limitation can be somewhat complicated.

Self-employed workers report expenses for business use of the home on Form 8829, and then the allowable expenses carry over to Schedule C.

Employees report expenses for business use of the home on Schedule A as unreimbursed business expenses, which are miscellaneous itemized deductions. They are deductible only to the extent that they, together with other miscellaneous itemized deductions, exceed 2% of adjusted gross income.

Sale of Your Principal Residence

When you sell your home, the entire gain may not qualify for the $250,000 / $500,000 exclusion that is normally available upon the sale of a principal residence. You will be taxed on the depreciation that you deducted after May 6, 1997, on the business portion of the home.

Conclusion

Years ago, deductions for home offices were considered to be a red flag. Some people who qualified were reluctant to claim the deductions because they thought it might trigger an audit. Now, however, home offices are common, due in part to the inexpensive technology which greatly increases the amount of work that can be done from a single room. Social changes have also contributed to the proliferation of home offices, as retirees, young mothers, and even students set up businesses at home. But like any other deduction, these expenses are open to challenge in the event of an audit. So, keep good documentation to show business use of the office area.

Vacation Homes

The best tax benefit to owning a vacation home is the potential for tax-deferred appreciation of the property. No income tax is due on the appreciation in value until you sell your vacation home, and at that point, the gain may qualify for the lower capital gain tax rates.

And there are two strategies you could use to avoid capital gain tax on the sale of your vacation home. First, you could make the property your primary residence for two of the five years before the sale, which could qualify you for a non-taxable gain of up to $250,000 if single and $500,000 if married. (This exclusion is discussed more fully in the Homeownership chapter.)

Not able to convert the property into your primary residence? You may still be able to dodge the tax bullet when selling your vacation home by using a like-kind exchange. Even if you have used the property for family vacations, you probably held it for investment purposes as well. After all, you didn't buy the property expecting it to drop in value, did you?

Current Deductions

What about benefits that can reduce the costs of your vacation home right now? As discussed in the Homeownership chapter, property taxes and mortgage interest you pay on your vacation home can be deductible when paid.

A Boat as a Home

A boat has been defined as a hole in the water that the owner pours money into. No doubt, boating is an expensive hobby. But if your boat qualifies as a second home, the interest you pay on your boat loan can be deductible, which could significantly reduce your boating costs.

To qualify, your boat must have sleeping, cooking and restroom facilities. Also, there must not be any legal prohibition against using the boat as a home, such as zoning restrictions.

Mixed Use

Many vacation homeowners rent their properties *and* use them personally. So, IRC Section 280A has divided vacation homes into three types:

Personal use property is rented 14 days or less, and is not considered rental property. Rent income is not taxable, and expenses related to the rental are not deductible.

Rental property has personal use of not more than 14 days or 10% of the days the home is rented at fair rental value, whichever is greater. All rental income is taxable and expenses are allocated between rental and personal use. Owners may deduct a loss from the rental activity, subject to the passive activity loss rules.

Mixed use property has personal use exceeding the 14 day/ 10% limit. All rental income is taxable. Expenses are allocated between rental and personal use. Rental deductions cannot exceed gross rental income, with unused deductions carried forward to future years.

For mixed use property, gross rental income equals the total rental receipts reduced by expenses of obtaining tenants such as advertising and realtor fees. Note that rents reported on Form 1040, Schedule E may be different than gross rental income for purposes of figuring the deduction limit. On Schedule E, gross rental income does not exclude certain expenses such as advertising and realtor fees.

A personal use day is any day that the property is used by the owners, family members, or someone who pays less than a fair rental price. Donating use of the home to a charity also counts as personal use.

If a property falls under the mixed use rules, deductible expenses cannot exceed gross rental income. To determine what to deduct, expenses other than advertising and realtor fees must be allocated in the following order:

1. Expenses that are allowable regardless of the rental activity such as qualified mortgage interest, property taxes, and casualty losses.
2. Rental expenses that do not affect the basis of the property, such as insurance, utilities, management fees, repairs and maintenance.
3. Expenses that affect the basis of the property, such as depreciation. (But remember that some of the cost basis is attributable to the land, and land cannot be depreciated.)

These limits don't apply to a dwelling unit that has been rented out for a consecutive period of at least 12 months that begins or ends in the tax year, or less than 12 months that begins in the tax year and at the end of which the unit is sold or exchanged. During this "qualified rental period," the unit must be rented, or held for rental, at fair market rent.

There are also special rules for mortgage interest deductions on vacation homes. If you already own a first and second home, the non-rental portion of mortgage interest on a third residence may be considered nondeductible. Or, it may be considered investment interest expense, which is deductible to the extent you have investment income.

If a vacation home is a second residence with rental use of 14 days or less, the mortgage interest is fully deductible on Schedule A. If a vacation home is a second residence with rental use greater than 14 days, qualified mortgage interest is still fully deductible even if other rental expenses are suspended under passive activity loss rules.

Strategy Tip

If rental deductions are limited by gross rental income, consider taking out an equity loan on your principal residence. Use the loan proceeds to retire the debt on the vacation home. Interest on the equity loan will generally be deductible as personal residence interest, and more deductions will be allowed for rental expenses.

Conclusion

A vacation home can produce current deductions, but the real investment and tax benefit may be the rapid tax-deferred appreciation.

Rental Real Estate

Back in the good old days, investors rushed into the real estate market to take advantage of generous tax benefits and quick appreciation. But, the Tax Reform Act of 1986 made the decision to invest in rental real estate more difficult. However, real estate still offers plenty of tax benefits and opportunities for leverage and rapid appreciation. Commercial and residential properties are currently available, and mortgage interest rates are low.

Rental Income and Losses

Cash basis taxpayers, which includes practically all individuals, must report rental income in the year it is received, or constructively received.

Deductible expenses include advertising for tenants, mortgage interest, repairs, cleaning and maintenance, property taxes, insurance, management and other professional fees, depreciation, and utilities.

You can also deduct travel expenses incurred in managing or maintaining your rental property. For your mileage, you may deduct actual expenses or use the standard mileage rate.

Although the cost of repairs is deductible when paid, the cost of improvements must be capitalized and depreciated over a number of years. So, the question always comes up: how do you tell the difference between repairs and improvements? The answer is: it depends! Actually, it really does depend to some extent on how aggressive you and your tax advisor want to be. But, to over-simplify, repairs get the property back into the condition it was in previously, and improvements make it better than it was previously.

To protect your deductions, go to the trouble to keep good records of all rental receipts and expenses.

Passive Activity Loss Rules

The passive activity loss (PAL) rules were designed to limit the benefits of tax shelters, including rental real estate. Generally, passive activity losses can offset only passive activity income.

Unused passive losses are "suspended" and carried forward to subsequent years until passive income is generated. Once you dispose of the activity, losses that are still suspended become deductible. Note that an "activity" may include one or more properties.

Although all rental activity is considered passive, an exception to the PAL rules is allowed for losses from rental real estate activities in which the owner actively participates during the year. A loss of up to $25,000 may be deducted against other income, including wages and portfolio income, by individuals with adjusted gross income (AGI) of $100,000 or less. The allowance is phased out between $100,000 and $150,000 of AGI and is disallowed for individuals with AGI exceeding $150,000.

Active Participation

To qualify for the $25,000 rental loss allowance, the owner must actively participate during the tax year. Also, the owner must have at least a ten percent ownership in the property, and his or her interest must not be that of a limited partner.

Active participation does *not* require regular, continuous and substantial involvement in the operations. However, the owner must participate in a significant way by making management decisions or arranging for others to perform services for the rental property. Qualifying management activity includes approving new tenants, setting rental policies and terms, and approving capital expenditures or repairs.

Self-Rented Property

There are some unusual rules that apply to real estate that is leased to a related business. Generally, income or losses from rental real estate is considered to be passive. However, the IRC § 469 regulations state that net rental income is treated as not passive if the property is rented for use in a trade or business in which the owner materially participates. The material participation clause essentially makes the property "self-rented."

The IRS wants to prevent you from using self-rented property to create passive income in order to utilize passive losses from other activities. Pursuant to the passive activity regulations, in any year that net income is generated, the income is treated as income not from a passive activity. In a year that a loss is generated, the loss is treated as passive, creating a double-edged sword effect.

However, suspended passive losses from self-rented property can be used against net income from the same property in later years.

Exception for Real Estate Professionals

Rental real estate is generally treated as passive, regardless of the owner's level of involvement. As a result, if rental realty produces a tax loss, its owner generally cannot use the loss to offset non-passive income (such as wages, dividends or interest).

Qualifying real estate professionals can benefit from an exception to the PAL rules. If you qualify and you materially participate in the properties, losses generated by those properties are not treated as passive. That means you can use the losses to offset non-passive income (such as wages, dividends, or interest). Material participation means substantial and ongoing involvement under one of a number of tests carried in IRS regulations.

Material participation is achieved by meeting one or more of the following tests for each activity:

- putting more than 500 hours into the activity,
- providing substantially all participation in the activity,
- putting more than 100 hours and as much participation as anyone else into the activity,
- showing "significant" participation in the activity,
- providing material participation for five years,
- providing personal service activity and materially participating for three years, or
- using other facts and circumstances to show material participation.

In determining whether the above tests are met, married individuals are able to count the participation of their spouse.

If material participation is achieved, the time commitment test must also be met to qualify as a real estate professional. This requires that you meet two requirements on an annual basis. First, more than 50% of the personal services you perform must be in real property trades or businesses in which you materially participate. Second, more than 750 hours of your personal services must be performed in real property trades or businesses in which you materially participate. Real estate businesses can include building, rebuilding, buying, renting, operating, managing and leasing realty, as well as realty brokerage businesses. Married individuals cannot combine their time to meet the time test.

Like many exceptions to tough tax rules, the real estate professional's exception carries a number of complications. For example, consider these two important points:

First, if you do not meet the above tests, you can aggregate all of your rental real estate activities and attempt to meet the material participation and time tests by treating all such activities as one activity. However, caution should be used when making this election because activities that are grouped together cannot be disaggregated until they are entirely disposed. In addition, meeting the real estate professional test in one year does not guarantee the same result for future years. In other words, the aggregated properties could generate passive losses in the future.

Second, a property in which you are a material participant in one year could carry suspended losses from years in which you didn't qualify as a real estate professional. This type of property is treated as a former passive activity. That means the suspended losses can offset only income from the activity that produced the loss, or passive income from other investments. In general, the suspended losses cannot be used to offset nonpassive income until the property is sold.

Depreciation

Real property improvements and furnishings are eligible for depreciation. Land cannot be depreciated.

Property placed in service now is depreciated using the

modified accelerated cost recovery system (MACRS). Rental real estate is depreciated over 27.5 years if residential, or 39 years if non-residential, using MACRS straight-line depreciation.

Tangible property other than real estate is generally depreciated over five to seven years, depending on the type of property, using MACRS 200% declining balance method. Furniture and kitchen appliances, for example, may be depreciated over five years.

For example, let's say you purchase a residential duplex this year for $100,000. You might treat $10,000 of the purchase price as your cost basis in the land and treat the other $90,000 as your depreciable basis in the structure. Using straight-line depreciation over 27.5 years, your depreciation expense in the structure would be $3,273 per year. If you purchased kitchen appliances separately for the rental, you would depreciate these items over 5 years using MACRS 200% declining balance method. Under this depreciation method, depreciation deductions are accelerated in the early years. (Be sure to see the Cost Segregation chapter.)

Immediate Deductions

If your property is typically rented for seven days or less at a time, it may be treated as "transient" rental property. This means that the Section 179 election may be available. This election allows an immediate deduction for up to $100,000 of property placed in service during the year. Real property does not qualify, and personal property normally does not qualify if used in rental real estate. However, transient property is treated more like a business (i.e. a hotel) than rental real estate for this purpose. So, personal property used in transient rental property may qualify. This could include appliances, furniture, fixtures, and decorations, for example.

Nontax Considerations

Many factors should be considered before investing in the rental market, including:

Who will manage the property?
Is it in a desirable location?
Is there a good market for renting the property?
Will the property appreciate in value?
Will this type of long-term investment meet your
    financial objectives?
Can you afford to carry the property during vacancy
    periods?

Leverage

One of the strong incentives for investing in rental real estate is the opportunity for leverage. Let's say you've found a $100,000 duplex in a growing community. You buy it, putting 10% of the purchase price down and borrowing the other $90,000 from a bank. You rent the property to tenants, and use their rent payments to fund debt service and other expenses of the property. If after one year the property has appreciated 10%, you've doubled your money. This is because you put only $10,000 of your money into the property and have realized tax deferred appreciation of $10,000.

Disposition

Selling your property a few years down the road could create a sizable tax liability since the property's value may have increased yet your basis has decreased due to the depreciation you deducted. But the income tax bite can be deferred through a like-kind exchange or an installment sale. Also, remember that the taxable gain on disposition may be partially offset by prior year losses that are still suspended due to the infamous passive loss rules.

Conclusion

Rental losses can offset up to $25,000 of nonpassive income each year for individuals who actively participate in the management of the property and whose adjusted gross income falls below $100,000. The $25,000 allowance is phased out for the investor with AGI between $100,000 and $150,000. Unused losses carry forward to subsequent years. There are some exceptions to these rules and you should consult with your tax advisor about your particular situation.

In addition to the tax benefits, substantial returns are available to the careful investor who finds the right property *and* a good tenant.

Segregating Costs

When you purchase or build a building, please don't assume that the entire cost must be depreciated as real estate. You may be able to accelerate some depreciation deductions by segregating the costs between the real property (depreciated over 27.5 or 39 years) and personal property (depreciated over perhaps 5 or 7 years).

The larger deductions will reduce your taxable income in the earlier years, but it will also mean lower deductions in later years. Due to the time value of money, reducing your taxes in the short run is usually best.

A building used in business operations is typically depreciated over a 39-year period. (Residential property may be depreciated over 27.5 years.) But, some of the components in the building may qualify for shorter depreciable lives. If you segregate the cost of the building into tangible personal property and the actual building structure, you can depreciate the cost of the personal property on shorter lives.

Personal property may include telephone systems, lighting, carpets, vinyl coverings, and electrical systems. Separating the costs of these properties allows you to use the applicable depreciation method for each individual asset. These assets have depreciation periods of between 3 and 10 years. This allows you to take larger deductions in the earlier years of your building than if you depreciated everything at a 39-year rate.

Example

James purchased a commercial building for $1,000,000. He estimates that $100,000 of the cost is attributable to the land, which is not depreciable. The other $900,000 could be depreciated over 39 years, allowing just $23,077 of depreciation deductions in a typical year. However, James determines that a computer system purchased with the building qualifies for a shorter life. He can deduct the $50,000 cost of that system over five years, instead of over 39 years.

This strategy works best for a business that has a mature income stream. If you expect your business income to rapidly increase in the years following the purchase of the building, and are in a low tax bracket right now, it may be better to keep your deductions spread over a longer period. You will recognize more income in the early years when it will be taxed at a lower rate, but reduce your income in the future when it would be taxed at a higher rate.

Conclusion

Cost segregation should be considered any time you purchase or construct a building, because 39 years is a mighty long time.

The Family Farm

Keeping Grandpa's farm in the family may provide you and future generations a great place for rest and relaxation.

The farm can create tax benefits, too. Consider, for example, tax deferred appreciation of the property. And deductions for insurance, labor, utilities, maintenance, depreciation, property taxes, mileage, supplies, feed, vehicle expenses, licenses, fertilizers and chemicals, fuel, interest, subscriptions, and professional fees.

The Hobby Loss Rule

Under Internal Revenue Code Section 183(a), generally, no deductions are allowed for an activity that is not engaged in for profit. This is known as the hobby loss rule, and means that losses from hobbies, such as raising horses for enjoyment, are not deductible. According to IRC Section 183(b), expenses related to hobbies are deductible only to the extent of income from the hobby. This allows you to offset hobby income, but not create a loss from a hobby.

A farming activity is presumed to be an activity engaged in for profit if the gross income derived from the farm for three or more of the taxable years in the period of five consecutive taxable years exceeds the deductions related to the farming activity. Once this presumption has been met, the burden of persuasion will shift to the IRS. However, if you cannot make a profit in three out of five years, you still may be able to deduct your losses by showing other evidence of your profit motive.

In numerous court cases, taxpayers have been allowed to deduct losses because their farms were operated in a businesslike or professional manner. Maintaining good books and records, consulting with experts, changing operating methods to improve profitability, and devoting time and effort to the farm help demonstrate businesslike and professional operations.

Another indicator of profit motive can be the anticipation of the property's appreciation. IRS regulations state that "the taxpayer may intend to devise a profit from the operation of the activity, and may also intend that, even if no profit from current operations is derived, an overall profit will result when appreciation in the value of land used in the activity is realized since income from the activity together with the appreciation of land will exceed expenses of operation."

However, the IRS may try to divide the holding of farmland and farming operations into two separate activities. If the IRS succeeds, you may not be able to use land appreciation to offset your farm's operating losses in proving profit intent.

But there are several ways for your farm to generate cash revenue, which not only helps demonstrate a profit motive, but also helps pay the property's upkeep. Consider the sale of crops, livestock, timber, and hunting rights, for example.

The Passive Loss Rules

The passive loss rules are complex limitations on deductions from "passive" activities. Passive activities include ventures that you have invested in, but do not "materially participate" in. The idea is to prevent you from deducting losses from activities that you simply invest in.

Our tax laws require you to pay tax on gains from your passive activities. But losses may be used only to offset passive income. Any excess passive losses are suspended and may be carried forward and deducted in a later year when you have passive income. Any losses still suspended when you sell the activity may then be deducted against other (non-passive) income, such as wages, dividends, interest, and pension distributions.

So, if you do not materially participate in the farm activity, a net loss from your farm will be deductible only against passive income. Material participation in a farm is achieved by meeting one or more of the following tests:

> Putting more than 500 hours into the farm activity,
> Providing substantially all participation in the farm activity,
> Putting more than 100 hours and as much participation as anyone else into the activity,
> Showing "significant" participation in the activity,
> Providing material participation for five years,
> Providing personal service activity and materially participating for three years, or
> Using other facts and circumstances to show material participation.

In determining whether the above tests are met, a married individual is allowed to count the participation of his or her spouse.

Timber

Growing timber has tax advantages that are not available with other farm products. First, there is a reforestation credit. The credit is 10% of your reforestation expense, up to a maximum annual credit of $1,000. This credit is available each year in which you incur reforestation expenses.

Also, up to $10,000 of reforestation expense you pay each year can be amortized (deducted) over a period of 84 months. However, that $10,000 expense must first be reduced by half of the reforestation credit you claim that year. This means that up to $9,500 can be amortized over 7 years. Any amount of reforestation expenditures over the $10,000 becomes your basis in the timber, which will eventually reduce your taxable gain on the sale.

Example of Reforestation

Suppose you spend $12,000 this year to have seedlings planted. Your reforestation credit will save you $1,000 of federal income tax. You will also get to begin deducting $113 each month for 84 months (that's $10,000, minus half of the $1,000 credit, divided by 84 months). The other $2,000 of cost basis in the seedlings will be used to reduce your taxable gain when the timber is sold.

Capital Gain Treatment of Timber

Another tax advantage to growing timber instead of other crops is in the timing and character of income you must recognize. With crops, you would have to pay taxes on any profit each year. This profit would be taxed at your marginal tax rate as ordinary income. With timber, you do not have to pay tax until you choose to sell it, and the gain can qualify for the lower capital gain tax rate.

Like-Kind Exchange of Timber

It may also be possible in some states to defer the tax on timber gains by using a like-kind exchange. This is possible where standing trees are considered to be part of the real estate under local laws. The value of the real estate should appreciate with the growth of the trees. Therefore, you may be able to sell real estate with standing trees, and acquire other real estate, without current taxes. (Please see the chapter on like-kind exchanges.)

For More Information on Timber

Visit *www.TimberTax.org* which is maintained by Purdue University and the U.S. Department of Agriculture.

Fuel Credit

When you purchase fuel at the pump, you pay federal taxes that are included in the price of the fuel. This tax revenue is intended to pay for the construction and maintenance of public roads and highways.

If you use the fuel off-road, you are entitled to a credit for the taxes paid at the pump. This credit is claimed on IRS Form 4136, which is filed with the farm owners' income tax return. The amount of the credit varies between 18 and 25 cents per gallon for gasoline, gasohol, aviation gasoline, diesel fuel, and kerosene.

Developing the Land

If it comes to the point where you want to develop the land, there are strategies you can use to minimize your tax liability. For example, the land may have appreciated greatly before you even begin development. But when you develop it and sell parcels, you will be treated as a dealer for tax purposes and the profit will be considered ordinary income (not capital gains). This means your gains will be taxed at your top (marginal) federal rate. To the extent that the property appreciated before you begin development, you should find a way to qualify that gain for the lower capital gains rate (the maximum federal rate is 15%).

For example, it may be possible to create an S corporation and sell the land to that corporation before development begins. This will allow you to treat the gain as long term capital gain. The S corporation can then develop and sell the land. Profits from development will be taxed as ordinary income. However, you will have saved up to 20% tax on the original appreciation of the land.

Conclusion

To show that your farm is an active, for profit business, keep proper records and books, showing sales on a consistent basis. Consult with experts, and devote substantial amounts of personal time and effort to the operations.

Conservation Easements

Contributing a conservation easement on undeveloped land can create a current income tax deduction for you, without requiring your family to give up use or ownership of your property.

Donating an easement involves gifting all or a portion of your property rights to a qualified organization, such as a land trust. This usually includes the right to develop the property.

This strategy especially appeals to those who want to keep land in the family long term, and don't expect to ever fully develop the property anyway. You can reserve, among other rights such as forestry, recreation and education, "conservation" development rights; or you may wish to reserve just a few single family residential lots.

The idea is that you donate the legal right to develop your property to a charitable conservation organization. That charity won't develop your property since that's what these conservation organizations hope to prevent. But that legal right has value, and since you are donating something of value to a recognized charity, you are entitled to a deduction.

How Do I Qualify?

Under Internal Revenue Code Section 170(h)(4)(A),

a qualified conservation easement must be exclusively for one or more of the following purposes:

a) Preservation of land for outdoor recreation by, or the education of, the general public;
b) Protection of a habitat of fish, wildlife, or plants, or a similar ecosystem;
c) Preservation of open space, including farmland and forest land, for the scenic enjoyment of the public or pursuant to a clearly delineated governmental conservation policy, provided preservation will yield a significant public benefit; or
d) Preservation of a historically important land area or a certified historic structure.

The conservation purpose must be protected in perpetuity. But the easement does not need to open your property to the public. And you can retain certain rights, as mentioned above.

Any interest you retain must be subject to legally enforceable restrictions that prevent your retained interest from being used inconsistently with the conservation purpose. This would not necessarily prevent you from farming a portion of the land, cutting timber, or using the property for hunting and other personal reasons.

The donation of the perpetual conservation restriction would give rise to an immediately vested property right in the conservation organization. If you later sell the land, the conservation organization may be entitled to a share of the sale proceeds proportionate to the value of the easement at the time of the gift.

How do I get my Deduction?

To determine the value of an easement, a "before and after" appraisal methodology is generally used. Under this method, the amount of the contribution deduction is the difference between the fair market value of the property before and after the contribution. But you must have owned the property for more than a year in order to deduct more than your cost basis.

If your property is owned by an S corporation, family partnership or LLC, the tax benefit of a charitable contribution would be passed on to the shareholders, partners or LLC members.

Individual taxpayers can offset up to thirty percent of their adjusted gross income with a "non-cash" deduction of this type. C corporations can offset only ten percent of their taxable income in any year. But both individuals and corporations can carry any excess deduction forward to the next five years, and deduct it subject to those same income limitations. So, you and your family may continue to realize income tax savings in years following the donation.

Some states offer incentives as well, such as tax credits for landowners putting property under conservation easements.

The easement can also result in property tax savings and estate tax savings, since it reduces the market value of the property.

Conclusion

The conservation easement fits well into the plans of property owners who need current tax deductions and want to preserve the beauty and conservation values of their property for their grandchildren's grandchildren.

Like-Kind Exchanges of Real Estate

The like-kind exchange is still one of the most effective tax planning tools available to real estate owners. This vehicle allows owners to complete the sale of one property and reinvest the sale proceeds in another property without current taxable gain.

This benefit is available to individuals, partnerships, corporations and other entities that own real estate used in a business or held for investment. The like-kind exchange can defer gain brought about through appreciation in value, as well as through depreciation claimed on tax returns over the years.

Internal Revenue Code Section 1031 provides for the rollover of sale proceeds without current recognition of taxable gain. To comply with this section, strict regulations must be followed (as if you didn't already know that). Under Section 1031, non-recognition of gain or loss generally is mandated if property held for productive use in a trade or business or for investment is exchanged solely for property of a like-kind that is to be held for productive use in a trade or business or for investment.

Regulations under Section 1031 are designed to accommodate owners of real estate who wish to sell their property and then purchase replacement property from a third party. As a practical matter, one property is usually sold and another purchased on a later date. This is known as a deferred like-kind exchange. A common method of accomplishing the exchange involves a "qualified intermediary" who assists in effecting the sale and the subsequent purchase. (Isn't the lingo fun?)

Three very important requirements in the regulations involving the exchange are:

1. Your new (replacement) property must be identified within the "identification period," which is the 45 days following the date you sell your original property.
2. The replacement property must be acquired within the "exchange period," which is the 180 days following the sale of your original property.
3. You must not be in constructive receipt of your sale proceeds during the exchange period.

Requirements for Identifying Replacement Property

To qualify as like-kind, the replacement property must be identified by the end of the identification period, which ends 45 days after your original (relinquished) property is sold. It's important to note that every day counts toward that forty-five day limitation—including Saturdays, Sundays and legal holidays.

You may need to use an option, lease, or purchase contract with a future or contingent closing date to be sure that the property you want will be available.

The identification requirement is met only if your replacement property is designated in a written document you sign and send to an unrelated person. The document may be hand-delivered, mailed, faxed, or delivered by other means.

The description of the property must be unambiguous. A legal description or street address will suffice. The identification requirements are designed to be specific enough to preclude you from later substituting another similar property for the one you originally identified.

If the replacement property is to be constructed, IRS regulations require that the identifying description provide "as much detail as is practicable at the time the identification is made."

Any identification may be revoked before the end of the identification period. A valid revocation must be contained in a signed document sent to the same person who received the original identification notice. A new replacement property would then need to be identified by the end of the identification period.

Identifying Alternative Replacement Properties

It is possible to identify several alternative replacement properties. However, if more than one potential replacement property is identified within the replacement period, one of three tests must be satisfied. The first is the three-property test. This rule permits you to identify up to three alternative properties as replacement property.

The second test is the 200% test. Under this rule, an unlimited number of properties may be identified so long as their aggregate fair market value does not exceed 200% of the fair market value of your relinquished property.

The third test is the 95% test. If too many properties are identified so that neither the three-property test nor the 200% test can be satisfied, you must actually receive at least 95% of the aggregate fair market value of the identified properties within the 180-day exchange period. Meeting this test would, of course, require a significant amount of cash or other consideration from you, in addition to the relinquished property.

Obviously, meeting the requirements for the identification of replacement property is much easier if the entire sale proceeds will be rolled over into a single replacement property.

A special rule provides that "incidental" property is not counted as separate property and does not need to be separately identified. Incidental property is defined as property that is (1) worth less than 15% of the aggregate of the replacement property and (2) typically transferred together with the larger item in standard commercial transactions. This rule may provide that the furnishings of a hotel, for example, do not need to be separately identified in meeting the identification requirement.

Requirements for Receiving Replacement Property

You must acquire the replacement property by the *earlier* of: 1) the 180th day after the sale or 2) the due date of your tax return (including extensions) for the year in which the sale occurs. Under IRS regulations, the replacement property is considered to have been received when the benefits and burdens test has been met. This test attempts to determine true ownership by focusing on which party benefits from the profits and bears the burden of losses associated with the property.

If your replacement property is to be constructed, it is important to note that only construction done by the end of the exchange period will qualify as replacement property. Any construction occurring after the exchange period will not be treated as like-kind property. Proper timing is critical.

For replacement property, you can purchase land and construct a building on it. However, construction on land that you owned before the exchange will not qualify as replacement property.

Requirement of No Constructive Receipt

It is very important to keep in mind that gain will be recognized in a deferred exchange to the extent that you actually or constructively receive money (or property not of a like-kind) before the replacement property is received. Actual or constructive receipt by your agent is considered to be actual or constructive receipt by you.

In structuring a deferred exchange you must consider several business risks associated with the transaction. Obviously, as the party ultimately receiving the replacement property, you will want control over the property selection and purchase arrangement, as well as security to ensure performance by the seller. Therefore, the regulations provide certain ways in which your sale proceeds can be handled while the purchase of replacement property is being arranged.

The sale proceeds can be kept in a qualified escrow account or a qualified trust, for example. You will not be in constructive receipt if the seller's obligation to provide replacement property is secured by cash or cash equivalent held in a qualified escrow account or in a qualified trust. Also, the regulations provide that a security or guarantee arrangement may be used. You will not be in actual receipt where the seller's obligation to provide replacement property is secured or guaranteed by a mortgage, deed of trust or other security interest (other than cash or a cash equivalent) or a third-party guarantee.

The regulations also provide for the use of a qualified intermediary to avoid actual or constructive receipt of cash or other property. A qualified intermediary cannot be a related party, however. The regulations state that a related party is one who has acted as your agent in the last two years including, for example, by performing services as an employee, attorney, or broker. However, for purposes of determining whether a person acts as an agent, the performance of services with respect to the like-kind exchange will be disregarded. Although this appears to be a contradiction, the regulations intend to provide that your intermediary in this transaction will not be considered a related party unless that individual conducts other business with you. A bank can be used as a qualified intermediary under certain circumstances.

To summarize the constructive receipt rules, it is imperative that the sale proceeds from your current property be held in a qualified escrow, or by a qualified intermediary or by another permitted vehicle until those proceeds are used to purchase your replacement property. If you (or an agent) have actual *or* constructive receipt of those proceeds prior to replacement property being acquired, the exchange will not come under Section 1031. At least to the extent of the amount actually or constructively received, your gain will be taxable. Remember, the IRS has no sense of humor.

The Reverse Exchange

The Internal Revenue Service usually approves a reverse like-kind exchange if it complies with a complex set of guidelines. In a reverse exchange, the property you wish to acquire is purchased before the property you want to give up has been sold. In addition to the requirements listed above, a reverse exchange must also meet the following conditions.

1. An unrelated person who qualifies as an "exchange accommodation titleholder" must hold the title to the new property from the date of acquisition until the date the old property is sold.
2. You must have a written agreement with the exchange accommodation titleholder indicating that the property is being held for your benefit to facilitate a Section 1031 tax-free exchange.

These requirements have similar time constraints to an ordinary like-kind exchange. You have 45 days to submit the identification letter from the time the accommodation titleholder (AT) purchases the replacement property, and the exchange should be completed within 180 days.

The AT is considered to be the owner of the property for federal income tax purposes, but the AT need not bear risks associated with the property. You may fund the purchase for the AT, and you may manage, use, and improve the property.

Planning Considerations

The regulations are rather generous in defining what type of property qualifies as like-kind replacement property. This is the area in which the law allows great flexibility. As long as your replacement property is real estate acquired to be used in a trade or business or held for investment, it can qualify. Therefore, you could sell an apartment complex or an office building and purchase raw land and a shopping center.

The replacement property should be acquired in the name of the same party that sold the relinquished property. If a partnership sold the old property, for example, that same partnership should acquire the replacement property.

If for any reason the identification requirements are not met, or the replacement property is not acquired within the exchange period, the gain will be taxable. Likewise, if some portion of the sale proceeds is rolled over properly and some portion is not, that portion not properly rolled over can generate taxable gain.

Basis

It is also important to keep in mind that under Section 1031 your basis in the relinquished property will become your basis in the replacement property. However, certain adjustments can be made to the basis of the replacement property. For example, if the replacement property costs more than your proceeds from the relinquished property, the additional purchase price will create additional basis.

Related Party Transfers

A special rule under Section 1031 will apply if the relinquished property is sold to a related party. The regulations provide that following an exchange involving a related party, taxable gain is triggered if either party disposes of the property it received in the exchange within two years after the date of the transfer. The gain would be taxable when the triggering disposition occurred.

There are, however, some important exceptions to this rule. A disposition during the two-year period will not trigger taxable gain in the event of the death of one of the parties, an involuntary conversion, or a transaction in which tax avoidance is not one of the principal purposes.

Boot

If you receive property that is like-kind and also receive property that is not, gain may be recognized to the extent of the unlike property's value. For example, if qualifying replacement property is received and also some cash or notes are received, the cash or notes would represent boot and would result in recognition of taxable gain. The assumption of liabilities can also be treated as boot. Therefore, if you sell property subject to a mortgage, and the buyer assumes the mortgage, you will be treated as having received boot up to the amount of that mortgage.

If the mortgage on your property is substantial, it will be important to plan for the appropriate treatment of that liability. If qualifying replacement property is acquired and the replacement property is subject to a liability, your assumption of the new liability may offset the fact that you were also relieved of a mortgage. Therefore, if the relinquished property is transferred subject to a mortgage, the two may offset each other in order to avoid triggering taxable gain. If the mortgage you assume is of a lower amount than the mortgage you relinquish, the difference between the two represents boot and will result in taxable gain. However, if the mortgage assumed exceeds the mortgage relinquished, the difference may create additional basis in your new property.

Reporting

The IRS provides Form 8824 for reporting like-kind exchanges. This form should be completed and attached to the property owner's income tax return.

State Treatment

When planning an exchange, the state income tax treatment should be carefully considered. The rules related to exchanges differ from state to state. Some states will not recognize the exchange as being tax deferred if the replacement property is located in a different state.

Conclusion

Internal Revenue Code Section 1031 and the regulations under that Section provide extensive requirements that must be met in order to achieve the benefits of a like-kind exchange. However, a like-kind exchange can result in the long-term deferral of a substantial tax liability. It is important that the regulations be followed *closely* and that each party be aware of these rules in order to complete the transaction properly. Be sure to use attorneys, agents, accountants and other advisors who are not only experienced with real estate transactions but are also familiar with the regulations under Section 1031.

Housing Credits

The low-income housing credit is one of the most powerful tax shelters currently available. In 1986, the federal government created this incentive to encourage the private sector to increase the supply of affordable housing. These credit programs have become a popular way to save taxes and to diversify a portfolio.

Individuals and corporations usually take advantage of the low-income housing credit by investing in a limited partnership. The partnership purchases or builds apartments that qualify for the credit. The apartments are occupied primarily by senior citizens. Then, the limited partnership allocates the available credits to the partners.

Unlike a deduction, a credit can directly reduce your federal income tax dollar-for-dollar.

The limited partnership typically provides a ten to twelve percent annual tax credit on the total investment. The partnership may not provide substantial operating income or losses, so the main attraction is the credits. However, if the partnership does generate a loss, the partners may use the loss to offset passive income. Also, the partnership may have either capital losses or gains on the ultimate disposition of the housing property, which will flow through to the partners.

Housing credits are generated for ten years. An individual can offset federal income tax on up to $25,000 of income annually, even if she has no passive income. Most credits have income phase-outs, but the housing credit is available to an individual regardless of his adjusted gross income. For example, if you are in the 35 percent federal tax bracket, you may use housing credits of up to $8,750 annually ($25,000 x 35%), even if you have no passive income. Corporations are not limited on the amount of credits which they may take, which is why many Fortune 500 companies have invested heavily in these partnerships.

The Fine Print

Investing in the limited partnerships requires a minimum of $5,000. The credits may not be used to reduce alternative minimum tax, and the credits are subject to the general business credits limitation. Any unused credits may be carried forward up to fifteen years, subject to the same limitations. In some circumstances, unused credits can be carried back to the preceding three years.

The limited partnership must operate the qualified housing for at least fifteen years. The law allows investors to accelerate the use of the tax credit over the first ten years. However, if the partnership does not continue to qualify for the credit for at least fifteen years, the investor is subject to recapture of the accelerated portion of the credits taken in previous years. This may amount to up to a third of the credits taken.

The investor could lose both his credits and initial investment if the project goes bankrupt. He or she may claim a capital loss on any amount of investment not recovered.

Example

The following illustrates the results for a hypothetical investor who puts $10,000 into a limited partnership that provides a ten percent tax credit. The three scenarios show no return of his initial investment, return of 100 percent of his initial investment, and return of 150 percent of his investment, when the property is sold.

YEAR		SCENARIO 1	SCENARIO 2	SCENARIO 3
	Investment	($10,000)	($10,000)	($10,000)
1	Tax Credit	$1,000	$1,000	$1,000
2	Tax Credit	$1,000	$1,000	$1,000
3	Tax Credit	$1,000	$1,000	$1,000
4	Tax Credit	$1,000	$1,000	$1,000
5	Tax Credit	$1,000	$1,000	$1,000
6	Tax Credit	$1,000	$1,000	$1,000
7	Tax Credit	$1,000	$1,000	$1,000
8	Tax Credit	$1,000	$1,000	$1,000
9	Tax Credit	$1,000	$1,000	$1,000
10	Tax Credit	$1,000	$1,000	$1,000
11		$0	$0	$0
12		$0	$0	$0
13		$0	$0	$0
14		$0	$0	$0
15		$0	$0	$0
	Total Credits	$10,000	$10,000	$10,000
	Return of Principal	$0	$10,000	$15,000
	Total Return on $10,000	$10,000	$20,000	$25,000

In the above scenarios, the investor put in $10,000 up front and then saved $10,000 of federal income tax through credits, regardless of how much cash he received when the property was finally sold.

Planning Tips

If you invest in a limited partnership that passes credits through to you, be aware that the partnership may not file its tax return before April 15th. If you do not receive your Schedule K-1 from the partnership by April 15th, you will need to request an extension of time to file your tax return.

To decrease risk, it is wise to invest in limited partnerships that have already been allocated the housing credits and are nationally diversified.

Conclusion

Like any other investment, careful thought should go into any decision to participate in these credit programs. Their long-term nature can be viewed as a disadvantage or as an advantage. These investments are not liquid, but provide tax credits for ten years.

Private Annuities

Want to transfer valuable property to a relative without paying huge estate or gift taxes? The private annuity is a type of installment sale that may be just your ticket.

The property is sold at its fair market value, and the buyer begins making periodic payments of principal and interest to the seller. The seller receives fixed payments over his or her lifetime, but the remaining receivable immediately cancels upon the seller's death.

The seller (annuitant) may also opt to defer receipt of the annuity payments for a period of time. For example, you may plan to retire in ten years and would like to begin receiving payments at that time. You would incur no tax consequences during the period prior to the receipt of payments. The deferral period is not limited.

The amount that must be paid in the annuity contract is computed by using the appropriate actuarial tables and discount rates.

The payments are scheduled so that, if the seller lives to exactly his or her life expectancy, he or she will have received fair market value for the property, plus interest on the installments. So, if the seller lives exactly to whatever his or her remaining life expectancy was at the time of the sale, the buyer ends up paying fair market value.

If the seller dies prematurely, the payments stop and the buyer has received a bargain. If the seller lives beyond his or her projected life expectancy, the buyer overpays for the property.

Private annuities avoid gift taxes because there has been a sale, not a gift (as long as the property was properly valued).

Since payments stop at the seller's death, there is no receivable to be included in the seller's taxable estate.

This strategy also allows for a deferral of capital gains tax and the tax on depreciation recapture, because these taxes are paid only as the payments are received. Capital gains on an unsecured annuity are recognized proportionally with receipt of each payment. Therefore the gain is not fully recognized until the seller reaches the age found in the actuarial tables. It is important to realize that there are no IRS penalties or interest on these deferred tax payments.

Basis

The buyer's basis in the property for determining gain, should disposition of the property occur prior to the death of the annuitant, is the total of the annuity payments made under the contract plus the value of the prospective payments under the contract. The basis for determining loss would be the total of the annuity payments actually made through the date of disposition.

At the death of the seller, the buyer's basis in the property is then adjusted to the total of the annuity payments actually made under the contract.

Please note that the basis step-up will not be available upon the seller's death since the property will not be included in the seller's estate.

The Risk

The private annuity is usually used to sell property to a close family member. This is because the buyer's obligation to make the annuity payments is unsecured, and because of the huge gamble involved. If the seller sells to his own descendents, and then dies prematurely, he has achieved his goal of transferring his property to his heirs without gift tax or estate tax, and with minimal capital gains tax. But if he had sold to an unrelated party and then died prematurely, he would have lost some of the family wealth.

General Steps in Planning a Private Annuity

Decide what property is to be sold. Income-producing property works best since the buyer will want to receive cash from the property to fund the annuity payments.

Determine who the buyer(s) will be. Family members and trusted associates are the most appropriate since the buyer's obligation to make the annuity payments is unsecured.

Estimate the fair market value of the property to be transferred.

Determine the seller's basis in the property.

Look up the seller's life expectancy and the applicable interest rate published by the IRS.

Calculate the annuity payment, and determine whether

the annuity property will provide the buyer with enough after-tax cash flow to make the required annuity payments. (When necessary, other methods can be used to ensure adequate cash flow to the buyer, such as gifts or compensation from the seller.)

Complete the sale and then be sure that the buyer makes the periodic payments as scheduled.

Example

Due to failing health, a business owner is ready to retire and transfer the business to his daughter. He wants to turn it over to her immediately but does not want to pay the $3 million of capital gains taxes that would be incurred by a cash sale. He also wants to avoid gift tax and the 50% estate tax.

He transfers the business to his daughter in exchange for a private annuity which is scheduled to begin monthly payments to him in three years. His life expectancy is 25 years according to the tables.

The daughter will use a combination of business profits, compensation from the business, and loans from the business to make the monthly annuity payments to her father.

Of each annuity payment that the father receives, a portion will be a tax-free return of his basis and a portion will be capital gain, as determined by his life expectancy at the time the annuity payments began. The rest of each payment will be interest income, taxable to him at ordinary income tax rates.

No portion of the annuity payment made by the daughter will be deductible as interest expense. However, in determining basis upon the father's death, the entire amount of the annuity payments made create basis for the daughter. Depending on the nature of the property, the daughter may be able to depreciate the property.

After receiving payments for two years, the father passes

away. The daughter will make no further payments. She has acquired the business, and there is no gift or estate tax to be paid.

Selling to an Unrelated Buyer

There is a way to get the tax benefits of a private annuity even if you sell to an unrelated person.

Set up a trust and transfer the property to the trust in exchange for a private annuity contract of equal value. Be sure to transfer the property to the trust before any third-party sale is negotiated. Then the trustee can sell the property to a buyer for cash. The trust has little or no taxable gain since it paid fair market value for the property, and then sold it for fair market value.

The trust then invests the sale proceeds, and begins making periodic annuity payments to you, at the time you want to begin receiving payments. Note that you could defer the first annuity payment for a number of years, allowing the trust's investments to grow. Please keep in mind, however, that the trust will pay income tax on its earnings each year. A trust is taxed at the highest federal income tax rate when taxable income reaches a relatively low amount. The trustee will want to consider this when deciding on the type of investments held within the trust.

One thing that you should be aware of is that you are not allowed to serve as trustee of the trust. You are not allowed to have any direct control over the trust. An adult trust beneficiary or any person independent of you would be allowed to serve as trustee. Your spouse is not allowed to be trustee nor is your spouse allowed to be a beneficiary of the trust.

Upon your death, the trust terminates and the cash and investments remaining in the trust go to the trust's beneficiaries, who could be your children, your grandchildren, your favorite charity, or the brilliant author who told you about this strategy.

Conclusion

The private annuity is a powerful way to quickly move a significant amount of value out of an estate without triggering huge capital gains taxes or gift taxes. It works best with a profitable business or income-producing property, so the buyer has an income stream to fund the purchase payments.

Captive Insurance Companies

What does a captive insurance company have to do with reducing income tax? You may have never even heard of a captive, but this chapter will provide an overview of captive insurance companies and describe what they can do for you.

What is a Captive Insurance Company?

A captive insurance company is a private insurance company that is set up to insure some of the risks of a parent company, a group of related companies, association members, or industry group. It is a tax-advantaged way to self-insure risks that you choose to insure. Captive insurance companies are an alternative to traditional insurance arrangements. They are "captive" companies, meaning that the owners control them.

The Financial Benefits of Setting up a Captive Insurance Company

Fortune 500 companies have benefited from captive insurance companies for years. But now, small businesses and investors are realizing financial and tax benefits by establishing their own insurance companies.

A partial list of potential advantages includes:

> Lower insurance costs due to low overhead and no sales commissions,
> Control of the level of risk assumed and premiums paid,
> Control over claims,
> Coverage tailored to meet specific needs,
> Accumulation of investment income to help pay claims,
> Control over cash flow,
> Potential protection of company funds from predatory lawsuits, and
> Reduction of income taxes.

Due to rapidly increasing insurance costs, this may be a practical way to obtain some lower cost insurance. This could avoid premium escalations related to the recent poor investment income of traditional insurers. For example, a business may reduce its premiums by accepting a large deductible on a policy, and then obtain coverage for that deductible from its own captive.

What are the Tax Benefits of Setting up a Captive Insurance Company?

The tax benefits described in the following paragraphs pertain only to bona-fide insurance companies. The benefits vary depending on the size of the insurance company.

Small Captives

You've heard charities described as "Section 501(c)(3) organizations." Section 501(c)(3) of the Internal Revenue Code says that a qualifying charity does not have to pay federal income tax. Other organizations may also be exempt from federal income tax under Section 501(c), such as homeowner associations, labor unions and political parties.

What few people notice is that a small insurance company can be exempt, under 501(c)(15). This section of the Internal Revenue Code provides that an insurance company (other than a life insurance company) with gross receipts of less than $600,000 and premium income representing more than 50% of the gross receipts each year, is treated as a tax-exempt organization. Unlike most other exempt organizations, an individual, a company or an association can own these insurance companies.

If you qualify under section 501(c)(15), your captive can earn up to $600,000 of income each year without paying any federal income tax. Unfortunately, the gross receipts of related companies are included in the $600,000 limitation. This rule limits the use of these types of captives in coordination with other operating businesses. However, the small captive can still be useful in certain circumstances. A better solution is usually to use a larger captive.

Large Captives

If your insurance company has premium income of less than $1.2 million, your company can elect for the premium income to be free of federal income tax. This provision is found in Internal Revenue Code Section 831(b). However, investment income earned on the funds held inside the insurance company would be taxable at ordinary corporation rates.

Businesses may pay insurance premiums on business policies issued to them by related insurance companies. If properly structured, the insurance expense is deductible by the operating business, yet the premium income is free of federal income tax to the insurance company.

Example

Ed is a successful real estate investor and business owner. He sets up a bona fide captive insurance company to help control his insurance costs and reduce income tax. He raises the deductible on his current insurance policies with traditional insurance companies. He insures the deductible amount through his captive. Once his deductible is higher, his traditional insurance premiums are $50,000 lower. That amount is paid to the captive to insure the deductible.

In addition, Ed obtains new types of insurance coverage from his captive insurance company, which he had not previously purchased from the traditional insurance company. These new coverages include business interruption, terrorism, and fire damage to his tracts of timber. His premiums for this coverage are $400,000. He doesn't mind paying the $400,000 because the cash will be held inside his captive insurance company.

Under Internal Revenue Code section 831(b), the $450,000 of premium income received by Ed's insurance company is free of federal income tax. Additionally, if his captive insurance company is properly structured, his operating businesses will be allowed to deduct the $450,000 as insurance costs. At a 40% (federal and state) income tax rate, this saved Ed's companies $180,000 of income tax.

Estate Planning

Captive insurance companies can help reduce estate tax as well. In the above example, if Ed's adult daughter owned the captive insurance company, Ed's businesses could pay premiums into the captive for legitimate insurance coverage. This would help reduce his estate because the cash would be transferred to the captive insurance company owned by the daughter. If we assume a 50% estate tax rate, the estate tax savings in the above example could be $200,000 (half of the amount paid for the new coverages).

In this example, the total potential tax savings for paying $450,000 into a captive insurance company could be as much as $380,000. The breakdown is: income tax savings of $180,000 and estate tax savings of $200,000.

The savings actually approach the cost of the $400,000 premiums on the new insurance coverage. And if no claim is filed on the business interruption, terrorism, or timber coverages, the $400,000 cash remains in the daughter's insurance company.

Words of Caution

Premiums between related parties must be properly structured in order for the premium payments to be deductible by the operating business. There must be risk shifting and risk distribution for the payments to qualify as insurance. The insurance company must also maintain sufficient third party insurance in order for premiums to be deductible.

Expenses to Set Up and Maintain

To qualify for the tax benefits, a captive must be a legitimate insurance company and comply with the regulations of the local jurisdiction. It is highly recommended that a company specializing in advising captive insurance companies be engaged. The insurance company must issue and account for its insurance policies, manage insurance risk, maintain proper books and records, provide reports to its owners and comply with various other laws regarding insurance companies.

These functions require a team of insurance, legal and accounting professionals. Establishing a small insurance company may cost as little as $25,000. Monthly management fees typically run at least $2,500. The cost of hiring a captive manager is usually less than hiring an employee who is capable of running all operations of an insurance company and the annual amount pales in comparison to the financial and tax savings that can be realized. For additional information regarding the setup and operation of a captive insurance company you may refer to www.primefortress.com.

Who Controls a Captive Insurance Company?

The owner controls the operations of the insurance company. However, an insurance management company usually performs day-to-day operations. The management company does not typically have direct access to the assets of the company.

How to Get Money from the Insurance Company

There are several ways for the owners to get cash out of the captive. The most common are salaries, loans, dividends, redemption of stock, payment of claims, and management fees to related entities.

It may also be possible to set up an LLC to own the captive's stock. The LLC could borrow from a bank, using the stock as collateral.

An individual owner may continue to hold the stock of his insurance company until his death, when the stock passes to his heirs with a basis step-up, and the company can then be liquidated without income tax.

Why set up a Captive Insurance Company?

Every business has its own risks and unique types of exposure. Consider setting up your own insurance company if you can no longer obtain the coverage you need at acceptable rates. Or, if you have risks that have a low probability of claims.

You may also wish to manage your insurance costs by assuming a limited level of risk, while obtaining reinsurance to limit your exposure.

Also, consider taking advantage of the long-term investment potential and significant tax savings that are available through a small insurance company.

This strategy is not right for everyone. However, if you are interested in controlling business insurance costs and saving income taxes, you should certainly evaluate the possibility of establishing a captive insurance company.

Over the past few years, South Carolina has emerged as a favorable state to domicile a captive insurance company. Other states, such as Vermont, have been the home of captive insurance companies for years. Many captives are set up offshore as well.

Conclusion

Over 4,500 companies and associations have established captive insurance companies. By doing so, they have been able to take advantage of cost savings, coverage not available through traditional insurance companies, and tax benefits.

The U.S. Virgin Islands Economic Development

Did you know that setting up shop on one of the U.S. Virgin Islands could mean a 90% reduction in federal income taxes for you and your business? This tax incentive is just one of the reasons why people are moving to the U.S. Virgin Islands. The beautiful islands have become more than just a vacation spot. They are now home to successful financial service entities, entrepreneurs and executives.

Life on the Islands

Residents of the U.S. Virgin Islands are subject to the same federal income tax that we are. They complete the same tax forms, but file their returns with the Virgin Islands Bureau of Internal Revenue instead of with the IRS.

Although they have the same tax laws as the mainland, the Virgin Islands have the authority to create economic development incentives and provide tax breaks for those who meet the requirements.

If you become a resident of the U.S. Virgin Islands and bring your business (or part of your business) with you, you may be eligible for some generous income tax savings under the U.S. Virgin Islands Economic Development Program (EDP). In 2003, there were approximately 95 active companies that were employing nearly 9,000 people and receiving benefits under the EDP.

This program, like many others intended to aid underdeveloped areas by attracting new business with special tax breaks, was made possible by Section 934 of the U.S. Internal Revenue Code. The program was originally written to attract manufacturing businesses, but was later expanded to include service businesses.

To obtain the benefits of this program, an official eighteen-page application must be filed with the Virgin Islands Economic Development Commission (EDC). The filing fee runs between $1,000 and $2,000 depending on the category of the applicant. U.S. citizens, domestic U.S. or Virgin Islands corporations, partnerships, limited liability companies, and trusts may all apply to receive the benefits under the EDP, but must agree to:

Provide full-time employment for at least ten individual

residents in the Virgin Islands who have been resident for at least one year prior to being hired;

Invest at least $100,000 in an industry or business that advances the economic well-being of the Virgin Islands and its people;

Be an active investor in the enterprise (as opposed to being just an agent); and Employ or contract for goods and services from businesses resident in the Virgin Islands for one year or more.

After filing the application, you must attend a public hearing, where you will be questioned about whether you will become a resident of the Virgin Islands as well as your expected philanthropic activities. The commission then grants you a certificate which serves as your contract with the Virgin Islands government providing for certain benefits if the above conditions are met. These benefits are for an initial period of 10 to 15 years, but may be extended for further ten-year periods as the business continues to promote further industrial and economic development.

The benefits are substantial: the U.S. Virgin Islands gives you a credit that reduces your U.S. income tax liability by up to 90%. There are a number of other tax benefits which may be available, as well, depending on the nature of your business.

How to Qualify

To benefit, you must qualify as a "bona fide resident of the U.S. Virgin Islands" by the end of the tax year. No provision in the Internal Revenue Code defines what is meant by a 'bona fide resident of the Virgin Islands' and the issue is being debated. The debate focuses on how much actual physical presence is required in the Islands and how to determine the individual's intent.

The Internal Revenue Service and the Virgin Islands authorities have each provided some guidance for defining residency, and recent court cases offer some help. However, these provide little guidance as to what will ultimately be ruled as 'bona fide residency.' We must still look to the specific "facts and circumstances" of each situation.

The following facts and circumstances may help demonstrate residency in the Virgin Islands:

> Establishing a well-furnished home in the Virgin Islands.
>
> Participating in social and cultural activities, such as joining a local church or country club.
>
> Being physically present in the Virgin Islands while working. The more time spent there, the better.
>
> The nature and extent of employment activities.
>
> The number and length of temporary absences from the Islands.
>
> Assuming economic burdens and paying taxes to the Islands.
>
> Being an Islands resident instead of a transient. This may include having a Virgin Islands drivers' license, registering to vote there, and owning a home comparable to the one previously used as a principal residence in the United States.
>
> Moving the family to the Islands.
>
> Good faith in making the move to the Virgin Islands.

However, if enacted, The American Jobs Creation Act of 2004 will require a resident to be present in the Virgin Islands at least 183 days per year.

How to Benefit

Income earned in the United States typically will not qualify for the credit. However, an American business owner may set up a management company in the Virgin Islands, and manage his profitable business from there. The management company would be entitled to reasonable management fees from the U.S. company for management services rendered. The management fees could be Virgin Islands income, qualifying for the tax credit.

The Risks

Because the tax benefits are so large, the Internal Revenue Service could be expected to look closely at whether you are in fact an Islands resident. And since there is no bright line test for residency, you could be at the mercy of the IRS and the ruling courts to ascertain your residency status.

This strategy has been manipulated by some unscrupulous parties but the strategy is still very effective for those who comply with the requirements and legitimately transfer their residency to the U.S. Virgin Islands.

Conclusion

To obtain these tax benefits, you must establish residency in the Virgin Islands. But, hey, there are a lot worse assignments than hanging out in the beautiful Virgin Islands. With the careful guidance of tax planning professionals, you may be able to reap the benefits of the U.S. Virgin Islands Economic Development Credit and transform your past spot for vacation into your future home of tax savings!

Long-Term Care Coverage

Long-term care insurance is becoming a popular benefit for employees. Here's why:

The cost of long-term care continues to rise rapidly, and Medicare benefits are available only for a maximum of 100 days.

Premiums for long-term care policies are still relatively low for healthy people.

Corporations can deduct the premiums for income tax purposes.

Employees are not taxed on premiums paid by the corporations.

Employees are not taxed on benefits paid to them (or for them) by the insurance companies.

Discounts are available for employers paying premiums on multiple employees.

Coverage can be extended to family members, including non-working spouses (who are not eligible for disability insurance since they have no earned income).

When a covered employee leaves or retires, he can take his policy with him. Although the former employee would then pay his own premiums, he may still get discounted rates.

Coverage can be discriminatory. Companies can cover key employees without offering coverage to all employees. They can cover management but not administrative personnel, for example. (Discrimination cannot be based on religion, age, gender, race, etc.)

There are virtually no administrative costs to administer such a plan. (You have to love that part.)

Qualified Coverage

To qualify for the tax benefits mentioned above, policies must provide coverage only for qualified long-term care (LTC) services, be guaranteed renewable, and have no cash value.

Reimbursable services under current tax law include necessary diagnostic and preventive care as well as therapy and rehabilitation. They also include maintenance and personal care services for individuals needing assistance with activities of daily living, as prescribed by licensed health care practitioners. (Still no word on whether being driven to the golf course qualifies as an activity of daily living.)

A qualifying policy will not cover expenses eligible for Medicare reimbursement unless Medicare is a secondary payer or the policy pays benefits without regard to actual expenses. In addition, tax laws prescribe consumer protection standards that must be met.

The important point is that not all policies are eligible for favorable tax treatment. But policies issued before 1997 are grandfathered into qualified status.

The Tax Advantages

Unfortunately, tax advantaged treatment is not available when the employer offers long-term care benefits under a cafeteria plan or flexible spending account arrangement. (The value of coverage funded under such an arrangement would be included in the employee's taxable income.) However, employers can offer long-term care insurance to all employees paid for via after-tax employee payroll deductions. Also, Archer medical savings account or health savings account funds can be used to buy LTC insurance.

Partnerships, limited liability companies (LLCs), and S corporations can pay and deduct premiums for their owners. But the owners must treat that as a taxable benefit to themselves, and then deduct it on page one of their personal income tax returns. The owners still get the benefit of deducting the premiums; it's just a different way to get there.

Due to a recent law change, most self-employed workers can now deduct 100% of the premiums they pay for themselves and their dependents.

Those who don't get coverage from an employer and are not self-employed can purchase their own individual policies. They can deduct their premiums as medical expenses on Schedule A (Itemized Deductions) of their personal income tax returns. But to do so, their total medical expenses for the year must be high. Only the portion of their total medical expenses that exceeds 7.5% of their adjusted gross income is deductible.

Deductions for premiums are subject to dollar limits based on the insured's age.

Benefits from qualifying policies are 100% tax free if paid under an expense reimbursement policy to the extent daily benefits don't exceed $230 (unless actual costs are also higher).

Conclusion

For employers to stay competitive, LTC insurance should be considered as a tax advantaged way to provide meaningful benefits to key employees. Group LTC plans generally cover employees, spouses, and most relatives. A separate policy may be needed for each individual, but multiple policies may qualify for a discount.

Mature self-employed workers should consider this coverage to protect themselves, especially since they can now deduct the premiums and receive qualifying benefits without tax.

Frequent Flyer Miles

The Internal Revenue Service taxes just about everything, but there is one tax-free benefit that you can easily use. Many credit card companies offer incentives, such as frequent flyer miles. Cardholders can earn these incentives without having to pay income tax on their value.

To earn more frequent flyer miles, you could use a designated credit card for business purchases, including office supplies, inventory and equipment. The company would pay the bill for all business-related purchases, but you would receive the frequent flyer miles since the card would be in your name. By using a credit card for larger purchases such as equipment or inventory, for example, you can accumulate frequent flyer miles rapidly.

Example

Mary is a dentist in a small town. Since she enjoys traveling, she uses a designated credit card for purchases of dental supplies, medical equipment, and some of the office's utilities. Since these are significant expenses and they recur every month, she always has plenty of frequent flyer miles. She uses those miles to get free airline tickets and discounts on hotels and car rentals whenever she's ready to take her family on vacation.

The View from the IRS

The Internal Revenue Service originally said that frequent flyer miles earned by employees on *business* travel were potentially taxable. But due to strong objections from taxpayers and the airlines, the IRS said they would not attempt to tax this as a fringe benefit. They don't want to face significant compliance issues, such as determining the value of the miles, and whether the miles would be taxed when earned or if and when used.

If your company (rather than the airline or credit card company) provided the frequent flyer miles to you, they would be taxable to you.

Caution

Be sure the company pays the full balance each month soon after the bill arrives. This will help you protect your credit rating, and avoid high interest rates and debt accumulation.

You may need to use more than one card if there is a cap on miles that can be earned. If you sell the miles, which can be done through a broker, the sales proceeds will be taxable.

Conclusion

To get this tax-free benefit, get a credit card that offers such an incentive and use it only for business purchases. Have the company pay the bills. Then, take your family (and your tax advisor) to Hawaii.

Business Autos

Do you use a vehicle primarily for business? If so, there are several major tax implications that should be considered. However, the first question that needs to be answered when acquiring a new vehicle is whether to purchase or lease. Buying and leasing have significantly different tax consequences.

Purchase

If you decide to buy, the luxury auto limits can present a significant problem. However, you can qualify for a substantial income tax benefit by buying a vehicle that is a 'qualified non-personal use vehicle' (QNUV).

Specifically, you may be able to:

Use the Section 179 election to deduct up to $100,000 of the vehicle's cost in the year that you purchase the vehicle; AND

Qualify for faster depreciation than what is available for "luxury autos." The IRS defined a "luxury auto" as a vehicle costing more than $14,800 in 2004.

A QNUV is defined as a vehicle with a manufacturer's gross vehicle weight rating (GVWR) above 6,000 pounds that is used in a business.

A QNUV may also be a vehicle with a GVWR of 6,000 pounds or less that, by reason of its design, is not likely to be used more than a small amount of time for personal purposes.

Under the new regulations, a vehicle that is 6,000 pounds or less is no longer subject to the luxury automobile depreciation and expensing limitations, if its design can confirm its primary business purpose. For example, a van that weighs less that 6,000 pounds but has only front bench seating, with permanent shelving that fills most of the cargo area, that constantly carries merchandise or equipment, and that has been specially painted with advertising or the company's name would qualify as a QNUV.

Also, because of new tax legislation, buying *new* vehicles for business can qualify for an additional 50% depreciation if purchased before January 1, 2005. This is not available when buying used vehicles.

However, if enacted, The American Jobs Creation Act of 2004 will limit the Section 179 deduction on these vehicles to $25,000.

Example

The following scenarios illustrate the significant income tax benefits, which you may be able to use by purchasing a business vehicle that qualifies as a QNUV.

Frank buys a used vehicle in 2004 that he will use 100% for business. The vehicle costs $36,000.

If Frank's vehicle is not a QNUV, it will be subject to the "luxury auto" depreciation rules. In the first year, he is limited to deducting the *lesser* of 20% of the cost of the vehicle or $2,960. Therefore, Frank is able to deduct only $2,960 of the vehicle's cost in 2004. Because of the "luxury auto" depreciation limits, it will take another 18 years to fully depreciate the cost of the vehicle.

If Frank purchased the same vehicle *new* instead of used, he is allowed an additional $7,650 of depreciation in the first year. He would be able to deduct $10,610 of the vehicle's cost in 2004, and it will take another 13 years to fully depreciate the cost of the vehicle.

If Frank's vehicle qualifies as a QNUV, it will not be subject to the luxury auto limits. So Frank can elect to claim a Section 179 deduction on his vehicle and deduct the full $36,000 in 2004.

As you can see, there is a substantial difference in the amounts that Frank may deduct depending on whether or not the vehicle qualifies as a QNUV. If it qualifies as a QNUV, he may deduct $36,000 of the vehicle's cost in 2004. If not, he can deduct only $2,960 if used or $10,610 if new in 2004. These deduction amounts are the maximum deduction based on 100% business use. If business use is between 50 and 100%, the allowed deduction is calculated by multiplying the maximum deduction times the business use %.

Leasing

Another way to avoid the luxury auto limits on depreciation is to lease a business auto, rather than buy it. Leases are subject to an inclusion rate on any vehicle that costs more than $17,500, but the inclusion rate is much less severe than the luxury depreciation limit, especially in the first two years of the lease. The longer a car is leased the less of an advantage leasing has in terms of avoiding the luxury auto limits.

As in buying a vehicle, expenses must be deducted in proportion to business use. If the auto is used 90% for business, then 10% of each lease payment is non-deductible. (Just to warn you, it's very difficult to convince an IRS agent that a Corvette is used 100% for farm business.)

To partially offset the lease deduction on a luxury auto, there is an income inclusion amount that must be taken into account. A table in the IRS regulations shows the inclusion amount, based on the value of the vehicle at the beginning of the year. In past years even after adding in the income inclusion amount, leasing a business auto provided better deductions than buying. However, with the additional first year bonus depreciation available for 2004, a lease payment would have to exceed $884 on a new automobile for the lease deduction to be more than the depreciation deduction for the first year. For the second year and beyond, the lease would provide a better deduction. If trying to determine the better alternative for a new auto in 2004, it would be best to consider the length of time you plan to drive this auto.

As with other decisions, you should consider the whole picture and not just the tax benefits. For example, buying a vehicle when zero percent financing is available may be a better overall financial decision than leasing. Personal preferences and needs must also be considered. How many miles the vehicle will be driven will play a huge factor in whether it is more beneficial to buy or lease. If the vehicle will be driven over 15,000 miles per year, it most likely would be a better option to purchase the vehicle, because there is usually a charge of 8 to 15 cents for every mile driven over 15,000. The type of vehicle needed, the age preferred, the risk willing to be taken, and other factors will affect the appropriate decision.

Before a decision can be made to purchase or lease, it is important to be informed about the terminology and common hidden costs of leases. Understanding these terms may provide a valuable tool in negotiating a reasonable lease payment and avoiding hidden costs. Some of the major information to look for are the cap cost (vehicle cost, net of down payment), charges included in the monthly lease payment, and the lease-end residual value. This cap cost should be the same whether you purchase or lease the car. Before telling a dealer that you are considering a lease, negotiate the price. Then make sure that the negotiated price is used in calculating the lease payments. Also, it is important that you get a closed-end lease which establishes the vehicles value at the end of the lease, compared to the open-end lease, which leaves the value to be determined later. An open-end lease may result in you being held accountable for any difference.

Conclusion

The Internal Revenue Code offers a significant advantage for businesses that buy qualified non-personal use vehicles, because smaller vehicles are subject to the stringent luxury auto limits on depreciation. Leasing can also be an effective way of getting the greatest tax benefit out of business autos, especially when the leases are relatively short.

Examples of vehicles which may have GVWRs above 6,000 pounds:

AM General: Hummer

Cadillac: Escalade SUV

Chevrolet: Suburban, Tahoe, Astro (Cargo or Passenger) Van AWD, Express Cargo Van, Express Passenger Van, C 1500 Extended Cab, K 1500 Extended Cab, C 2500 Pickup, K 2500 Pickup, Crew Cab Pickup, Silverado Pickup

Dodge: Durango, Ram Van, Ram Wagon, Ram Pickup

Lincoln: Navigator SUV

Lexus: LX 470 SUV

Ford: Excursion, Expedition, Econoline (Cargo or Passenger) Van, F150 Super Cab Pickup, 4WD, F250 Pickup, F350 Pickup

GMC: Suburban, Yukon, Safari Passenger Van, Savanna Van, Sierra Pickup, Sierra Classic Pickup, Sierra Classic CrewCab

Land Rover: Discovery SUV, Range Rover SUV

Mercedes: M-Class SUV

Toyota: Land Cruiser

Always verify the GVWR, which can normally be found on a label attached to the inside edge of the driver's side door.

Employing Family

Certain business owners can experience significant tax benefits by employing their spouses and/or children.

Benefits

The potential tax advantage to employing your spouse or children is the opportunity for tax deductible benefits. Look for benefits that are deductible to the business, but not taxable to the employee.

For example, consider tax deferred retirement plans. The employee/spouse can contribute to a retirement plan and the business can contribute a matching portion to his/her account.

Example

A business paid the owner's husband $20,000 one year for his consulting services. The company had a 401(k) plan and would match up to 8% of each participant's salary. The husband deferred $11,000 of his compensation and the business contributed $1,600. The company deducted $21,600 and the husband was taxed currently on only $9,000.

Disadvantage

A disadvantage to employing a family member would be the FICA (payroll) taxes. These taxes could cost the company and the relative a total of roughly 12.5% of the relative's salary. (The payroll tax would be significantly less if the relative is already over the FICA wage base with another employer.) But remember, it may be to the relative's advantage to pay in to the Social Security system to increase future benefits.

Rules to Follow

To qualify for the tax benefits, there are a couple things you should remember. The family member must be a bona fide employee. You should be able to show that the services performed were meaningful. This does not preclude a relative who works part time from being considered an employee.

Another consideration is that any benefits provided to family must also be provided to other eligible employees. The top-heavy rules could limit contributions to a retirement plan.

Conclusion

Each situation is different. Run the numbers to see what the additional payroll taxes would be and how much income tax could be deferred.

Leveraging Equity

Do you have equity in your home or business? Would you like to put it to work for you earning tax-free income at an enhanced rate of return?

This strategy combines some of the techniques discussed elsewhere in this book. There are two ways to structure it depending on whether you use equity in a home or in a business.

Homeowners

Homeowners are allowed to borrow up to $100,000 against their principal residence on a home equity line of credit, use the loan proceeds however they like, and deduct the interest on that loan. You could use those proceeds to have a wild weekend in Las Vegas or you could use it to earn tax-free income.

Example

Sunny has plenty of equity in her home. She goes to the bank and establishes a line of credit. Currently the interest rate is 5%. She borrows $100,000 on her credit line and invests the proceeds in a flexible life insurance policy. (This policy must meet the seven pay test as discussed in the private pension chapter.) The policy is currently paying 7%. This creates a 2% interest rate spread. Keep in mind, the 7% is growing tax free and the 5% interest is tax deductible. If she is in a 30% tax bracket, the tax savings "enhance" the rate of return. After the tax benefit, her effective rate of earnings is 8.5% ((5% x 30%) + 7%). AND it is growing tax-free. (Remember the discussion earlier regarding the power of tax-free compounding?)

Estate Planning

This strategy can also be useful in estate planning. You could use a home equity line of credit to borrow against your home (which reduces the value of your estate) to fund a life insurance policy inside of an irrevocable life insurance trust. As discussed in another chapter, this special type of trust can provide tax-free income for your beneficiaries.

Business Owners

Business owners get even greater benefits from this strategy, since they are not limited to borrowing only $100,000.

This strategy is particularly useful inside of C corporations (where the corporation pays tax on its income and then the owners pay tax on the same income again when it is distributed to them in the form of dividends). This strategy uses loans from the business to fund an insurance policy that meets the seven-pay test as described in the private pension chapter. It is important to note that if the business borrows money to loan to the owner, the interest will probably not be deductible. However, if your business has cash, it can use its cash to make the loan to the shareholder who then invests in the flexible life insurance policy outside of the corporation. Then, in order to meet its short-term obligations, such as payroll or inventory purchases, the business borrows from a bank. It is important that the proceeds from the bank loan be traceable to the payment of legitimate business expenses.

Example

Mark is a business owner and is in the 40% tax bracket (combined federal and state). He borrows funds from his company at 5% and invests in a life insurance policy earning 7%. This results in an effective rate of return of 9% ((5%x40%) +7%).

Other Benefits

Two other potential benefits are:

This strategy can get equity out of a C corporation where it can be growing tax-free inside the life insurance policy for the benefit of the owner, key employees or their beneficiaries.

This may provide asset protection as the funds are removed from the operating business. In many states, life insurance policies are protected from creditors.

Implementing

This strategy is limited to closely-held companies since the Sarbanes-Oxley Act may prohibit loans to officers of publicly-traded companies.

Split dollar policies are often used in a business setting. This allows the business to receive back the amount it loaned to the owner or officer upon their death. However, the earnings while the policy was in force and the death benefit go to the officer/owner's beneficiaries. The cash value of the policy is used to collateralize the loan. Using a loan to finance a split dollar policy is sometimes referred to as the loan regime. It is one of two methods that can be used.

Doesn't Interest have to be Paid on a Loan?

The officer must "pay" interest on the loan. But he doesn't necessarily have to transfer cash back to the business. The interest could be calculated using the applicable federal rate and the amount could be added to his Form W-2 at the end of the year. This way he would be treated as if he received compensation from the business and used it to pay the business the interest it was due on the loan. The officer would recognize compensation income and the corporation would deduct salary expense. The income and deduction effectively offset each other.

What if I need Cash?

You can borrow against the cash value of the policy. Loans from life insurance policies are not taxable. You would not actually repay the loan or pay the accrued interest. Following your death, the beneficiaries of the policy simply receive the death benefit, less the loan balance and accrued interest.

Conclusion

Homeowners can access the equity in their homes and use it to produce tax-free income. And business owners can do the same thing on an even larger scale. When a business is involved, it is a little more complicated but can be well worth the effort.

Benefiting From State Apportionment

When a company conducts business out of state, it can easily establish nexus. Nexus is the minimum connection or contact between a taxpayer and a state sufficient to subject the business to the taxing jurisdiction of that state. Although this is not always unfavorable, it does add significant burdens in terms of record keeping and filing requirements.

Nexus can be created for income tax purposes if an entity derives income from sources within the state, owns or leases property in the state, employs personnel in the state in activities that exceed mere solicitation, or has physical or financial capital there. State law varies in the amount of activity or connection that is necessary to create nexus, but Constitutional principles, judicial doctrine and federal law, specifically Public Law 86-272, limit all states.

Federal Law

Under Public Law 86-272, states are prohibited from imposing a tax on net income when an entity's *only* connection with the state is the solicitation of orders or sales of *tangible* personal property, such as automobiles or office equipment, and such orders are approved and shipped or delivered from outside the state. When a company deals only in tangible personal property; it is protected under Public Law 86-272.

However, companies that deal in *intangible* personal property are *not* protected under Public Law 86-272. Therefore, the solicitation of the sale of intangible property or services may cause a company to create nexus within other states and require that the company file tax returns in those states.

Surprisingly, a company may *save* taxes by creating nexus in another state. If a company has nexus in at least two states, it is considered to be a multi-state corporation. The company files returns and apportions some of its income to those states. Most states use a three or four factor formula consisting of the ratio of sales, property, and payroll in the state to the *total* sales, property and payroll. (Sales may be weighted twice, thereby making it a four-factor formula.)

Example

Let's say ABC Company has nexus *only* in South Carolina. In this case, 100% of ABC Company's net income is taxed by South Carolina.

Next, however, let's say ABC Company is a multistate corporation with only 10% of its sales in South Carolina and 100% of its property and payroll in South Carolina. Only 55 percent of its net income is taxed by South Carolina [(10% + 10% + 100% + 100%) / 4].

Assume ABC also has nexus in one other state and 10% of its sales are in that state. The company may owe tax to that state on 5% of its net income [(10% + 10% + 0 + 0) / 4].

ABC is paying state income tax on only 60% of its net income (55% and 5%). The other 40% of its income may not be taxed by any other state. This result occurs because ABC has sales in states where it does not have nexus, and therefore does not have to file a state income tax return.

Sales Tax Caution

The nexus rules for sales tax purposes are not always exactly the same as those for income tax purposes. Once nexus is established in a particular state for sales tax, a company is required to collect and remit sales tax on sales of tangible property in that state. Payroll tax and other requirements may apply as well.

Activities That Usually Do NOT Create Nexus under Public Law 86-272

Advertising campaigns.

Carrying free samples only for display or distribution.

Owning or furnishing automobiles to salespersons.

Passing inquiries or complaints on to the home office.

Checking customers' inventories for reorder.

Maintaining a sample or display room for two weeks or less during the year.

Soliciting sales by an in-state resident employee, provided that the employee does not maintain a place of business in the state, including an office in the home.

Activities Usually Sufficient to Establish Nexus

Making repairs or providing maintenance.

Collecting delinquent accounts; investigating creditworthiness.

Installation or supervision of installation.

Conducting training classes or seminars for persons other than sales personnel.

Approving or accepting orders.

Picking up or replacing damaged or returned property.

Hiring, training, or supervising personnel other than sales employees.

Providing shipping information and coordinating deliveries.

Carrying samples for sale or distribution in any manner for consideration.

Owning, leasing, maintaining, or otherwise using any of the following facilities or property in the state: real estate; repair shop; parts department; employment office; purchasing office; warehouse; meeting place for directors, officers, or employees; stock of goods; telephone answering service; or mobile stores.

Consigning tangible personal property to any person, including an independent contractor.

Maintaining an office for an employee, including an office in the home.

Conclusion

The record keeping and filing requirements of a multi-state corporation can be laborious. (You need more paperwork to do, don't you?) Nexus can, however, significantly reduce a company's overall state income tax expense in the right circumstances.

Terminology and Concepts

Adjusted Gross Income (AGI) Adjusted gross income is the figure appearing at the bottom of page one of your personal income tax return. It includes all of your taxable income less certain deductions. This number is important because it dictates whether you are eligible for a number of tax benefits, including Roth IRA contributions and your full itemized deductions. Medical expenses, for example, are deductible only to the extent that, in total, they exceed 7.5% of your AGI each year.

Alternative Minimum Tax (AMT) The unpopular AMT is a second level of income tax, designed to ensure that everyone pays at least some tax. This purpose is accomplished by the fact that some items which reduce your taxable income do not reduce your taxable income for AMT purposes. Examples include state income tax, property tax and home mortgage interest. AMT now affects many middle-income people due to the fact that the AMT exemption has not been inflation adjusted.

Basis Your basis is the dollar amount assigned to an asset, which represents your cost or investment in the asset. When you sell an asset, such as stock, your basis in that asset is subtracted from the sale proceeds to determine the amount of your taxable gain or loss. When property is inherited, its basis is increased ("stepped up") to its fair market value.

Deduction or Credit? The difference between a deduction and a credit is dramatic. A deduction reduces taxable income, but a credit reduces tax *liability*. If your marginal tax rate is

28%, for example, a $100 deduction could save you $28. But a $100 credit could save you $100.

Depreciation Depreciation is the method of deducting your cost basis in a business asset which will last for more than a year. Because the asset is useful for more than a year, you generally cannot deduct your full cost in the year you buy it. You must deduct the cost over the assigned life of the asset. Depreciation lowers your basis in the asset.

Passive Losses Passive activities usually include business ventures that you have invested in but do not actively ("materially") participate in. Our tax laws require you to report any gains in these activities as current income, but any losses are suspended until you sell the activity or until you have passive income to offset them. Rental activities are generally considered passive, but there are some special rules that apply to real estate. (Please see the Rental Real Estate chapter for more details.)

Tax Avoidance or Tax Evasion? The difference, in theory, is simple. Tax "avoidance" is any process of legally deferring or avoiding tax. "Evasion" refers to any means of *illegally* deferring or avoiding taxation. Although it's easy to see the difference between the meanings of these terms, determining which term applies to a particular situation can be quite difficult.

Estate Tax The estate tax is imposed on the estate of a decedent based on the value of the estate's assets at the time of death. Assets left to a surviving spouse or to a charity are not subject to the tax.

The Double Taxation Dilemma

When you buy property or investments, be careful how you structure the ownership. The form of ownership will determine how income and gains are taxed, how much exposure the property has to estate tax, and how much legal protection the property has.

The most popular form of ownership for businesses and real estate is now the limited liability company (LLC). In most states, the LLC is treated as a corporation for legal purposes, providing some degree of liability protection to the owners. For income tax purposes, the owners (known as members) can elect how the LLC will be taxed. Most choose to be taxed as a partnership.

Partnerships report their income and expenses to the IRS each year on Form 1065. They divide the net income among the partners. Each partner receives a Schedule K-1, showing his share of taxable income. The partners are responsible for including their shares of income on their own returns and paying the tax. This is why the partnership is known as a "flow-through" entity.

If there is only one owner, he or she may set up a single-member LLC. This can provide the benefits of liability protection, but can also be a "disregarded entity" for income tax purposes. That means that the LLC does not file an income tax return, but is treated as a sole proprietorship for income tax purposes. The income and expenses are reported directly on the tax return of the owner.

A corporation can pay income tax on its profits or elect to be a flow-through entity. Tax-paying corporations are referred to as C corporations. Flow-through corporations are known as S corporations.

Large corporations are required to be C corporations, which is detrimental because their profits are subject to double taxation. The corporation pays tax on the income when the corporation earns it. Then the shareholders pay tax on the dividends when they receive them, although a maximum 15% federal rate applies (through 2008).

Owners of C corporations are interested in avoiding this double taxation. So, instead of dividends, they may begin to withdraw larger salaries, which are deductible at the corporate level.

Reasonable Compensation

The income tax laws allow corporations to deduct ordinary and necessary expenses incurred in carrying on their businesses. This includes compensation for services performed by shareholders and their family members, but only if the amounts are "reasonable" for the services performed.

A corporation paying excessive compensation to a shareholder-employee is required to reclassify the excess as a dividend (provided there are adequate corporate earnings and profits). This has unfavorable tax consequences to the company, since dividends are not deductible. This is where the double taxation comes in. Compensation is taxed only once—to the employee. This is important, since most business owners would rather spend three minutes in the ring with Mike Tyson than pay more corporate income taxes.

Whether compensation is reasonable depends on all the facts and circumstances. In general, compensation is considered to be reasonable if a similar amount was paid for comparable services provided by someone other than a stockholder. A true comparable, however, is rarely available.

Also considered is how much would be paid if the business were owned by an unrelated investor. After payment of all compensation, is there enough earnings left in the company to satisfy this hypothetical investor?

To determine a reasonable level of pay, many factors must be considered. For example, look at the input—long hours, special skills, and years of experience and education brought to the job.

Also look at the output, or the results achieved. After all, pay for any key employee should be performance based. Consider new customers and employees attracted to the company. Also consider steps taken to increase profitability, and similar accomplishments. Measuring one person's accomplishments can be difficult, however, since many things are accomplished through the efforts of several people working together.

Sometimes compensation for a particular year may include an amount for services performed in an earlier year. Business owners often receive reduced pay in the early years of a business, even though that may be when they worked the hardest. They also may not be adequately paid during periods of rapid growth, when cash flow is tight. They are entitled to catch-up pay later.

In addition to salary, benefits should be considered in determining whether compensation is reasonable. This includes pension and welfare benefits, as well as fringe benefits such as the use of a company car. An otherwise high salary might be reasonable if the benefits are less than those usually provided to a comparable employee.

Due to the potential adverse tax consequences, you should carefully document the reasonableness of your compensation. Explain how the amount was determined, and document the unique and valuable nature of your services.

If a year-end bonus is to be awarded, the terms should be written out in advance. The bonus may be some percentage of the increase in pretax profits over the prior year, for example. If any bonus is awarded, a resolution should explain why and when it was approved.

If you will be underpaid until a new business becomes profitable, and will receive proportionately larger pay later, perhaps this should be laid out in an employment agreement.

Paying the S Corporation Shareholder

S corporations, unlike C corporations, are tempted to keep the compensation of shareholder-employees low. This is because compensation is subject to payroll taxes but distributions to stockholders are not. (Either way, S corporation earnings are subject to income tax only once.) Federal and state tax authorities regularly review S corporations to ensure they pay enough payroll taxes on funds turned over to stockholders.

Pay reasonable compensation and keep records showing how compensation levels were set. Also, remember that decreasing your compensation may reduce the amount that can be put into your retirement account.

The Accumulated Earnings Tax

This brings us to the second method of avoiding double taxation on C corporation income. Some owners of closely-held corporations prefer to leave much of the earnings in the corporation as long as possible. This fuels the company's growth and defers tax on dividend income, with the possibility of it being taxed at capital gain rates whenever the company's stock is sold. (Or better yet, the second level of tax may be avoided altogether by using a charitable remainder trust or other vehicle described in this book to sell the company without taxation.)

In deferring dividends, beware of the accumulated earnings tax, which is really a penalty. It is designed to force profitable C corporations to pay dividends to their shareholders. The key to avoiding this penalty is documentation of the company's expected needs for capital. This includes plans for growth. The IRS cannot force you to pay a dividend, or penalize you, if you can show that your business needs the money.

When the IRS alleges that a C corporation has accumulated earnings above the reasonable needs of the business, it can impose an additional 15% tax on the "excess" earnings. Situations that are particularly ripe for challenge include those where a profitable corporation has a history of paying little or no dividends and has:

outstanding loans to shareholders or related parties, investments or assets having little relationship to the corporation's business, or large amounts of cash or liquid investments.

Corporations are generally allowed to accumulate up to $250,000 of earnings without having to prove why the accumulation is necessary. Corporate minutes are an excellent place to document the reasons why earnings in excess of $250,000 need to be retained by the company. It is important that the minutes be specific, spelling out precisely why the additional funds will be needed. Identify equipment that you anticipate needing to buy, for example. Whether you end up buying that particular asset may be irrelevant; the purpose is to show the IRS that your corporation is a developing company with a feasible plan for continued growth.

Conclusion

It is important to remember that the reasonable compensation issue and the accumulated earnings test are ongoing risks. An IRS challenge could come at any time. Therefore, corporate minutes and supporting workpapers should be updated regularly to minimize exposure to these potential penalties.

Both of the issues continue to pop up in audits of closely-held companies. Keep your guard up; keep good records.

Planning for Capital Gains

There is an important difference in the tax treatment of "ordinary income" and that of long-term capital gains.

Ordinary income includes wages, interest, pension benefits and just about all income other than capital gains. Ordinary income, other than qualifying dividends, is taxed at the escalating federal rates, which start at 10% and go up to 35%. A short-term capital gain may also be taxed at these rates.

Capital gains are derived by selling capital assets, such as stocks, bonds, and real estate. Through 2008, your long-term capital gains are generally taxed at a federal rate of 15%. (The long-term capital gains rate is only 5% if you are in the 10% marginal tax bracket.) Gains from the sale of real estate are taxed at 25% to the extent of depreciation claimed. And long-term capital gains from the sale of collectibles are taxed at a federal rate of 28%. Collectibles includes antiques, artwork and stamps, for example.

For long-term treatment, you must have owned the capital asset for more than a year before selling it. A year and a day is enough.

This rate differential is an important consideration. So, consider holding an appreciated capital asset until reaching the long-term point before you sell. Timing is always important in tax planning.

Also, keep the rate differential in mind in determining how to acquire new assets. For example, C corporations don't get the lower rate on long-term capital gains. This is one of the many reasons why real estate is not usually acquired in a corporation. Imagine selling some real property after holding it for several years and realizing a large gain. Suddenly you discover that your corporation will be paying 34% federal tax, and then you have to find a way to get the proceeds out of the corporation and into your own hands. A cash dividend from the company could be taxable to you at a federal rate of 15%, resulting in 44% of the gain going to Uncle Sam. Acquiring the real property in a flow-through entity, such as an LLC taxed as a partnership, would allow you to pay tax at the lower rate (15%), and pay only one level of tax, when the property is later sold at a gain.

Limitation on Deducting Losses

Individuals can use their capital losses to offset their capital gains, plus claim a deduction for another $3,000 of losses. This annual $3,000 limit is the same for married couples filing jointly and single taxpayers. Losses in excess of this may be carried forward and used in subsequent years, subject to those same limits.

Also, keep in mind that a loss must be *realized* to produce a tax benefit. This typically means that the capital asset must have been sold to an unrelated party. Unrealized losses, such as stocks that have dropped in value, do not produce a tax benefit until they have been sold and the loss realized.

Year End Planning

If you have capital gains, and don't want to pay tax on them, review your holdings before year-end. If you're holding losers, consider selling some of them to realize enough losses to offset your gains.

Wash Sale Rules

The government doesn't want you to sell a loser to realize the loss, and then immediately repurchase the same asset. If you repurchase the asset, or a substantially similar asset, within 30 days, the loss will not be recognized by the IRS.

Conclusion

The low rate on long-term capital gains provides plenty of opportunity to those who are paying attention. Remember that timing makes a world of difference.

Important Words of Caution

Of course, some tax strategies are not legitimate. A few of the more popular illegitimate strategies are discussed below, simply so you will know to avoid them! Remember that failure to report all of your income is a serious crime.

Offshore Bank Accounts

American citizens and residents must report their worldwide income to the IRS. However, the government believes that some people may be cheating by using foreign banks, especially those in the Caribbean. Since foreign banks do not have to report interest amounts to the IRS, someone could earn interest at a foreign bank and hope the IRS never finds out about it.

Offshore Credit Cards

The IRS believes that a few Americans are putting large amounts of cash into investment accounts at foreign banks. Those banks then issue credit cards to the account holders. These Americans use the credit cards to pay some of their living expenses here in the United States.

When the credit card bill is due each month, the foreign banks use current earnings from the cardholders' investment accounts to satisfy the bills.

These people intend to use this as a way to spend foreign

income in the United States, without reporting that income to the IRS.

Offshore Corporations

Another form of tax evasion being targeted by the Internal Revenue Service involves offshore corporations set up in tax haven countries. A business owner would establish an offshore corporation, supposedly to own equipment or an intangible asset, such as a copyright. The U.S. business then pays "rent" or "license fees" to the offshore corporation, thereby creating a deduction for the U.S. business. The business owner then uses a credit card for domestic living expenses, and at the end of each month, the credit card bill is paid by the offshore company.

Incorporating

Also, be cautious about those who recommend incorporating to save taxes. The fact that a personal expense is paid through a corporation does not make the expense tax deductible. And although many people are starting home-based businesses, saving taxes should not be a primary reason for doing so. Only *business* expenses are deductible through a home-based business, and it doesn't make sense to spend a dollar to save forty cents in taxes.

Conclusion

Please remember that tax evasion is a felony. If you receive a solicitation about these types of arrangements, you now know to avoid them. Some things are worse than paying taxes, going to jail is one of them.

Never rely on "hiding" techniques, and do not play the audit lottery. After all, you have many *legitimate* tax strategies available.

Also, you should not use any strategy solely for tax avoidance. There are multiple objectives that can be met by using any strategy described in this book. When you use any transaction that has significant tax consequences, document your reasons for the steps you take. These reasons may include estate planning, diversification of investments, business planning, and protecting your assets from predatory lawsuits.

Should We Have a Flat Tax?

You're probably just as fed up with the complexities of our income tax as everyone else. And you've heard plenty of presidential candidates promise to replace the income tax with a simple tax system. But, year after year, new laws are enacted that make our income tax even more complex and confusing.

After listening to many screaming taxpayers, I've concluded that there are four improvements that most people want in a new tax system. First, they want a tax that is fair. Second, they want a tax system that is less complicated than the one we have now. The third priority is encouraging people to save more of their income. And, finally, American businesses are looking for breaks to make them more competitive internationally.

Americans are also concerned about the federal deficit. And our leaders in Washington should realize that any tax overhaul plan must be revenue-neutral, meaning that it would be neither a tax increase nor a decrease.

Several interesting proposals have made their way into the press in recent years. A national sales tax and a value-added tax have been proposed, but the flat tax proposals have captured America's attention. Certainly, any of these proposals could have a dramatic impact on each of us. They could affect how we earn our living, how we save and invest, and how we spend our money. They could also significantly affect the value of our investments, and impact our employers, our governments, and our economy.

The overhaul proposals are only frameworks. Thousands of details need to be addressed before we can know how any of these proposed tax systems would work. Of course, the details are the heart of any tax system. Lots of proposals and theories sound appealing. But, as with our current income tax, "the devil is in the details."

Most of the popular flat tax proposals would tax individuals on salaries and wages, as well as benefits provided by employers. These taxable benefits could include contributions to retirement plans, life insurance coverage, and disability and health insurance coverage. The intent is to include *all* compensation in taxable income. But does it make sense to begin including group health insurance in taxable compensation? After all, the government wants employers to provide universal coverage, and one of the most effective ways to discourage something is to tax it.

Some flat tax proposals have included unlimited exemptions for interest, dividends, and capital gains. This would encourage everyone to save and invest. But, would it be fair? Imagine a factory laborer making $20,000 in one year. And consider a super-rich software mogul receiving a billion dollars in cash dividends and another billion in capital gains from stock sales that same year. Would the laborer in this example think it fair for her to pay more income tax than the software mogul?

The age-old problem of "what is wages?" could still be a difficult issue under a flat tax. Would employees still be taxed on personal use of a company car, for example? And would the IRS continue to audit family-owned businesses, looking for payments of personal expenses from company funds?

Of course, the biggest challenge now for the IRS is the widespread problem of unreported income. Would everyone who is paid in cash report it all under a flat tax?

And what about those who are self-employed? Suppose that after a long stint as an employee, you decide to make the big leap to self-employment. After all, having a business of their own is the American dream to many people. In your first year of self-employment, you may need to advertise extensively, and among other things, buy some office furniture and computer equipment. So let's say you have $50,000 of revenue that first year, and $50,000 of expenses. After just breaking even the first year, how much income tax should you owe? Should any of your business expenses be deductible? How many records should you keep to back up the revenue and expense figures you report? And wouldn't you be glad if I quit asking you so many questions?

Another critical issue is the treatment of foreign income. Some have suggested that income earned abroad be completely exempt from U.S. taxes. But this would not provide appropriate incentives. It would simply open the door to a whole new group of loopholes.

We need to carefully evaluate all of the side effects these changes could have. For example, if charitable contributions were no longer deductible, would colleges and charities become more dependent on taxpayer funding?

If mortgage interest becomes nondeductible, real estate values may drop significantly, creating a problem for mortgage lenders as well as for property owners.

Anyone owning a municipal bond would see its value drop, if interest earned from the bond became taxable.

And here's another issue with tax overhaul that bothers me. How would we transition from our current income tax to a new tax system? Change can be painful, and a drastic transition of this type could take many years and would surely have winners and losers.

Even if we made it through the long transition to a flat tax, people would still complain that they pay too much tax. They would still believe the government wastes their money. The flat tax proposals have not offered to lower our taxes or get us a better return for our money.

Still with me? Good. Now, the most critical issue of all. For several decades, Congress has used our tax system to encourage certain types of behavior, and to discourage other types. That is one reason why our tax code has become so complicated. There are thousands of tax incentives and penalties in our tax laws. Congress has used tax breaks to help American companies export their products, buy new equipment, and create jobs. Investors have been encouraged to fund low-income housing projects, help municipalities raise capital, and save for retirement. The list goes on and on.

If we had a "simplified" tax system, how would Congress encourage certain types of behavior, and how would they discourage other types? None of the tax overhaul proposals have given a comforting answer to that question.

Many of us would prefer that Congress not try so much behavior modification (aka social engineering). To those who want less government regulation, that has great appeal. But, after all these years, would Congress really stop trying to bring about desired changes in our society, our economy, and our businesses?

Perhaps a more simple and fair tax system can be created, somehow still including the most important incentives. A fairer tax, lower compliance costs, less government intrusion, and an increasing savings rate should be high priorities for us all.

Would a National Sales Tax be a Better Tax?

On the surface it seems like a good idea. Many people believe that they would pay less tax if we have a national sales tax instead of an income tax. However, the government will require the same level of revenue to operate regardless of the method of taxation. If someone pays less tax, someone else must pay more. While tax laws are an issue with most individuals, the method of taxation is not the only problem. For example, consider the problem of government spending.

While a national sales tax seems simple, there are a number of major factors that must be considered.

How much would the Sales Tax have to be?

Most estimates for a federal sales tax range from 23 to 30 percent. The states would have to increase their sales taxes also, in order to replace their lost income tax revenue. If a state already has a state sales tax, it may have to increase its sales tax to cover the lost state income tax revenue. We could end up with a combined (federal and state) sales tax of 40%. And remember, that is 40% of your gross purchases, not your taxable income (which is your gross income minus itemized deductions and personal exemptions). Such a sales tax would definitely change our buying habits.

Would the Internal Revenue Service go away?

Unfortunately, the answer is no. If we replaced the income tax with a national sales tax, the government would still need a large agency to enforce the collection of tax. There will always be those who try to circumvent the system and the IRS must be there to ensure that everyone collects and remits the tax properly. In effect, we could all be tax collectors for the government when we sell goods or services. But the IRS would be necessary to compel everyone to remit the tax they collect.

Cash Sales

A national sales tax would create many opportunities for tax evasion. Currently, the rate of income tax evasion is estimated to be around 15%. The current reporting requirements, which require that income be reported to Uncle Sam on a W-2 form or 1099 form, drastically reduce the rate of tax evasion. A sales tax would not have this type of cross reporting. Therefore, with a national sales tax, evasion rates much higher than 15% would be quite possible.

Cash sales would still be a huge enforcement problem. What about when you stop by a fruit stand on the side of the road? The farmer charges you for the fruit and adds a 40% sales tax to the price. You pay in cash. You, as the consumer, have paid the tax, which the farmer may never remit to the government. Under our current system, vendors may not report cash sales on their income tax returns, thereby cheating the government. But if they keep the sales tax that you paid, you will feel like they are cheating you.

What exactly would be Taxed?

Traditionally, most people think of sales tax applying to the purchase of goods, but not to services. If the entire taxing system were revamped, services would likely be subject to sales tax also. If they were not, the tax system could easily be circumvented. For example, your copier dealer might sell you a copier for $500 if you also buy a service agreement for $9,500.

So, what kinds of services are going to be taxed? (Most state sales taxes have many exemptions.) For example, would medical services be subject to the national sales tax?

Would there be other exemptions? What about college tuition? Would charities pay sales tax on their purchases? Many states require charities to pay sales tax now. Would childcare be exempt? Would there be exemptions for the costs of housing, clothing, food, nursing home care, or funerals?

How could we afford to pay sales tax when spending money that has already been subject to income tax? Changing the tax system could especially hurt retirees who have already paid tax on much of the money they are spending to live on.

Taxes are Political

Politicians are always trying to put a new spin on taxes. However, the bottom line is that taxes are a necessary evil. The government must have revenue to operate. The only way that taxes can really be lowered is if the government spends less.

However, there are many political issues that influence the tax structure.

Many lower income taxpayers pay no tax—some even get the Earned Income Credit, which is essentially a "refund" of money that they never paid in to the government. It is a redistribution of wealth. According to government statistics, the top 50% of income earners pay 96% of the income tax. The bottom 50% of earners pays only 4% of the total income tax. With a sales tax, would everyone pay at the same rate?

With a sales tax, starting a business could become more difficult since a large part of the tax would be paid right away, when equipment is purchased. With our current income tax, new businesses typically don't pay income tax until they get through the start-up period and become profitable.

A national sales tax could discourage spending in the United States. Why take the family vacation in Florida and pay sales tax on food, entertainment, lodging, fuel, etc? It would be too tempting to go to the Caribbean instead and save that 40%.

A national sales tax on consumption rather than net income could also discourage foreign investment in our country.

Who will have to Pay the Tax?

That is a good question and there are diverse opinions on this matter. If all businesses were subject to the national sales tax, there would be sales tax compounding. If a business purchases goods and then resells them, the sales tax would be paid twice on the same product. If a manufacturer sells to a wholesaler who sells to a retailer who sells to the end user, you could have three levels of tax.

If the sales tax were levied only on the end user, then who is the end user? What would prohibit someone from avoiding tax by consuming products that they purchased for resale? For example, a boat dealer could potentially avoid a large amount of sales tax by pretending to purchase a boat for resale, but using it himself instead. If a $20,000 boat escaped a 40% sales tax, the evaded amount would come to $8,000. This is another area in which enforcement would be critical.

Conclusion

At first, a national sales tax seems like a simple solution to reduce the complexity associated with the current income tax. However, there are a number of tough issues associated with a national sales tax. Even if we start over with a new tax system, within a few years, Congress will have created exemptions, preferences, exceptions, credits and rebates that will make it just as complicated as the previous tax system. To put it simply, a tax is a tax . . . no matter what you call it or how you collect it. And people will always look for ways to legally avoid a tax. But we do need a less complicated way to fund our government!

Asset Protection

An old tale says that the best way to get someone's attention is to whisper. But that's not true. Suggesting ways to save taxes is the surest way to capture anyone's attention. Don't believe me? Try it the next time you're at a funeral.

Lately though, another issue has become just as captivating, at least to business owners and others with wealth. That issue is commonly referred to as asset protection.

Everyone has heard scary stories about runaway juries and activist judges. As people lose their hard earned property to huge court awards, others are trying to prevent it from happening to them.

Clearly not all court orders are out of line, but who wants to gamble with the family fortune?

You don't have to be a lawyer to figure out that the first step in asset protection is to stay out of court. Unfortunately, that's not always possible.

Insurance is helpful, too. But, insurance policies come with a lot of fine print, and you know what that means. And having lots of insurance coverage may actually attract lawsuits, since predatory lawsuits are always aimed at deep pockets.

How about simply keeping your nose clean? That's a good idea too, but does it guarantee you won't ever be the target of a predatory suit?

Putting Property into Flow-Through Entities

Some asset protection techniques are relatively simple. Attorneys often recommend putting real estate into a family limited partnership or limited liability company (LLC), for example. This is one way to give up ownership without giving up control. Aside from powerful income and estate tax benefits, this may make property less attractive to plaintiffs. No one would want to sue, only to end up with a charging order against an interest in a family limited partnership. If he did, he may have to pay taxes on a portion of the partnership's income every year. He would not gain control of the property inside the partnership and could not force the partnership to distribute cash to him.

LLC operating agreements typically require the approval of other members for a new member to be admitted. A plaintiff may be awarded a charging order, which is similar to a judgment, but he may quickly become frustrated at not being able to force the LLC to distribute cash to him.

Equity Stripping

Another strategy some attorneys use is called equity-stripping. This involves keeping high levels of debt on property, so there is little equity for a plaintiff to target. Funds are borrowed against property and then put into protected vehicles.

Life Insurance, Annuities and Retirement Plans

Life insurance policies and annuities may, in many states, be protected by state law and therefore be less vulnerable to plaintiffs than other investments. Funds in qualified retirement plans, such as 401(k) plans, may be less vulnerable than IRAs.

Going Offshore

Other asset protection techniques are more involved, like putting property into a trust or LLC set up offshore. (These offshore entities are popular not only for asset protection, but can also be used to impress friends and relatives.)

A foreign entity can own property located in the United States. This can include the house you live in, the car you drive, and that prized collection of eight track tapes in the attic.

The idea is that the foreign jurisdictions may not recognize judgments of U.S. courts. So if you get a judgment against you for, say, $1 billion for selling cigarettes, your assets could be safely owned by an offshore trust or LLC.

Trustees will follow requests from the creator (grantor) in managing a trust. However, the trust agreement may state that the trustees are to ignore any request the grantor makes while under duress (i.e. after losing his or her shirt in court). So when the grantor instructs the trustees to turn property over to a plaintiff, that request would be disregarded.

A protector is often used to oversee the trustees. Various other techniques help ensure that the trustees don't mismanage the property or money.

These trusts also offer benefits in the form of privacy, but they are not tax shelters. Income earned by an offshore trust or corporation generally must be reported on the U.S. tax return of the grantor or owner. (Curses! Foiled again.) Even if not used for tax purposes, transfers to offshore trusts are subject to formidable IRS reporting requirements. And some transfers of appreciated property to offshore entities can trigger taxable gain immediately.

Caution!

These strategies are used to legally protect assets, but not to hide them. Attempting to protect assets from an estranged spouse, a bankruptcy court, or from any claim that is already pending can lead to serious trouble. Use asset protection strategies to protect yourself only from excessive claims that may arise in the future. And keep adequate insurance in force to cover reasonably anticipated liabilities.

Conclusion

This is a specialized and complicated area and should be undertaken only with the close guidance of reputable advisors experienced in this field. Asset protection planning, like income tax planning, is an on-going process which requires updates at least annually.

Updates

For complimentary updates on recent tax law changes affecting strategies discussed in this book, please visit:

MKBCPA.com

If you have suggestions for future editions of this book, please contact Stephen Kirkland at (803) 791-7472. Your thoughts will be appreciated.

Some Final Thoughts

The Bible speaks about our duties to obey the government, to pay taxes, and to love others. The following thoughts are from Romans, Chapter 13 verses 5 through 9.

Obey the laws, then, for two reasons: first, to keep from being punished, and second, just because you know you should. Pay your taxes too, for these same two reasons. For government workers need to be paid so they can serve you. Pay everyone whatever he ought to have: pay your taxes and import duties gladly, obey those over you, and give honor and respect to all those to whom it is due. Pay all your debts except the debt of love for others—never finish paying that! For if you love them, you will be obeying all of God's laws, fulfilling all His requirements. If you love your neighbor as much as you love yourself you will not want to harm or cheat him, or kill him or steal from him. And you won't sin with his wife or want what is his, or do anything else the Ten Commandments say is wrong. All ten are wrapped up in this one, to love your neighbor as you love yourself.

About Moore Kirkland & Beauston L.L.P.

MKBCPA.com
An independent member of BKR International

Moore Kirkland & Beauston L.L.P. is a full-service accounting firm, providing auditing, data processing, tax, and specialized consulting services to clients across South Carolina and in other states. The firm's five partners and 48 staff members are based in offices in Columbia, Charleston, Hartsville, and Greenville, South Carolina.

The firm's client base includes professional service firms, manufacturers, retailers, wholesale distributors, insurance companies and other financial institutions, dealerships, contractors, developers, and other businesses, as well as individuals, partnerships, and tax-exempt organizations.

We greatly appreciate our wonderful clients and our loyal, dedicated employees!

Index

Symbols

1031 exchanges 80

A

accumulated earnings tax 130
acquisition indebtedness 55
active participation 65
adjusted gross income 125
affordable housing credits 88
AGI 125
alternative minimum tax 17, 125
AMT 125
annuities 21
asset protection 36, 54, 119, 148

B

basis 86, 92, 125
boat as a second home 60
boot 87
business autos 111

C

C corporations 128
capital gains 133
   developing land 76
   home office 59
   principal residence 53
   timber 75

capital losses 134
   wash sale rules 134
captive insurance companies 96
charitable donations 46, 48
   easements 77
charitable lead trusts 51
charitable remainder trust 48
compounding 15
conservation easements 77
constructive receipt 83
convenience of the employer 58
cost segregation 70
Coverdell education savings
   accounts 28
credits 88, 125
CRT 49

D

deductions 125
deferred compensation plans 39
deferred like-kind exchange 80
depreciation 67, 126
   segregating costs 70
developing land 76

E

employing spouse or child 116
equity loans 55, 63, 117
equity-stripping 54, 149

estate tax 46, 99, 126
exchange accommodation
    titleholder 85

F

family limited partnership 149
farms 72
FICA taxes 116
flat tax 139
frequent flyer miles 109
fuel credit 76

H

hobby loss rule 72
home equity loans 55, 63, 117
home office 56
housing credits 88

I

identification period 81
incidental property 82
incorporating to save taxes 137
investment interest expense 55

L

leasing 113
leverage 54, 69
leveraging equity 117
life insurance retirement
    programs 39
life insurance trust 44, 118
like-kind exchanges 60, 79
    timber 75
limited liability company 127,
    149
LLC 127
long-term care insurance 106
low-income housing credits 88

M

material participation 66, 74
modified endowment contract 39
Moore Kirkland & Beauston
    L.L.P. 154
municipal bonds 17

N

national sales tax 143
nexus 121

O

office in the home 56
offshore bank accounts 136
offshore corporations 137
offshore credit cards 136
offshore entities 150
ordinary income 133
owner k plan 34

P

passive loss rules 64, 73, 126
    real estate professionals 66
    self-rented property 65
prepaid tuition programs 29
principal place of business 57
principal residence 53, 60, 117
private annuities 91
private insurance company 96
private pension 37
property taxes 55

Q

qualified conservation ease-
    ment 78
qualified intermediary 80, 84
qualified non-personal use
    vehicle 111

R

real estate professionals 66
reasonable compensation 128
reforestation credit 74
rental real estate 63
reverse like-kind exchange 84
Roth IRA 25

S

S corporations 130
sale of principal residence 53
   home office 59
Savings bonds 17
Section 179 68, 111
Section 412(i) plans 31
Section 501(c)(15) 98
Section 529 plans 29
Section 831(b) 98
segregating costs 70
self-rented property 65
small insurance companies 97
   benefits 97
   costs 100
state apportionment 121
supplemental life insurance
      plans 39

T

tax avoidance 126
tax evasion 126
timber 74
transient rental property 68

U

U.S. Virgin Islands 102
   qualifying for credit 105
updates 152

V

vacation home 60
variable annuities 21
variable universal life 41
Virgin Islands 102
   qualifying for credit 105
VUL policy 41

W

wash sale rules 135